C000131447

WALKING DOWN THE WYE

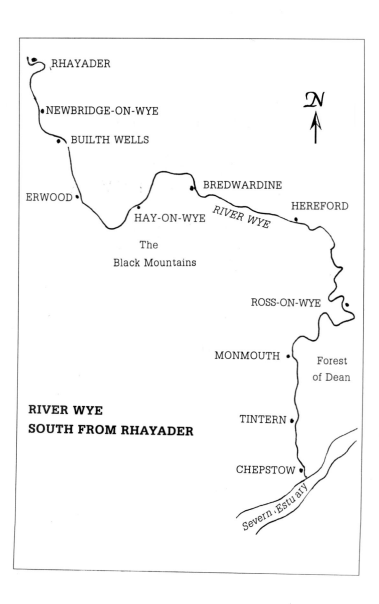

RHAYADER

NEWBRIDGE-ON-WYE

BUILTH WELLS

ERWOOD

BREDWARDINE

HEREFORD

HAY-ON-WYE

RIVER WYE

The
Black Mountains

ROSS-ON-WYE

MONMOUTH

Forest
of Dean

**RIVER WYE
SOUTH FROM RHAYADER**

TINTERN

CHEPSTOW

Severn Estuary

WALKING
DOWN THE WYE

The Wye Valley Walk
from Rhayader to Chepstow

by

David Hunter

CICERONE PRESS
MILNTHORPE, CUMBRIA

© 1992 David Hunter
ISBN 1 85284 105 2

British Cataloguing-in-Publication Data. A catalogue record for this book
is available from the British Library.

Advice to Readers

Readers are advised that whilst every effort is taken by the author
to ensure the accuracy of this guidebook, changes can occur
which may affect the contents. It is advisable to check locally on
transport, accommodation, shops etc but even rights-of-way can
be altered and, more especially overseas, paths can be eradicated
by landslip, forest fires or changes of ownership.

The publisher would welcome notes of any such changes

SKETCH MAPS: Vera Hunter
PHOTOGRAPHY: David & Vera Hunter

Front Cover: Penddol Rocks near Builth Wells

PREFACE

It should not be thought that a long distance footpath is the exclusive territory of those hardy backpackers who have both the time and stamina to set forth on a week or ten-day trip, camping out overnight or seeking the comforts of local inns, and day by day devouring the miles with enviable ease.

A long distance path should be all things to all men. The Wye Valley Walk's value as a continuous but not overly demanding route of 112 miles may be obvious but it has other attributes, possibly of much greater worth: a route from which further and wider explorations may be made, providing an introduction to immensely attractive but in a measure lesser known scenery such as mid-Wales.

The motorist heading into Wales from Kington cannot but appreciate the fine hill country that quickly envelops him. As he drives along the A44 making for Rhayader to start his tour of the Wye Valley he may make a mental note to look into the possibilities of exploring the Hergest Ridge for instance. Closer to the Wye Valley Walk is the lakeland created at the turn of the nineteenth century in the Elan Valley by the construction of the vast reservoirs with excellent walking and riding to be had along the bankside paths or over the hills. Further downstream the Black Mountains, part of the Brecon Beacons National Park, beckon seductively. Many miles further to the south as the river achieves full maturity the pleasures of the once remote Royal Forest of Dean are sampled. Scores of small towns and villages and a cathedral city all add to the rich mix.

There is scope for much flexibility in the discovery of the Wye Valley Walk, not just the one great pilgrimage, but a gradual uncovering in a series of weekends or day excursions spread over months or years. Public transport can be used to assist the exploration or where this is thin, taxi services may prove to be not that much more expensive than buses if there are two passengers. Friends or small groups walking day length sections can leave a car at each end, or by starting at different points may be able to swop their spare car keys (insurance cover permitting).

Those with a penchant for history or the picturesque; lovers of the world of nature, artists and photographers; people who believe that our countryside offers in miniature a landscape that compares well with anywhere else in the world; seekers of modest adventure, the hard-pressed looking for an escape from the everyday routine, or a different "unpackaged" holiday; all will find much along the Wye Valley Walk whether taken in large of small doses to satisfy their thirst or cure their ills.

The River Lugg at Mordiford. (Chapter 15)

CONTENTS

1: *The Wye and The Way*

The River Wye rises high on the slopes of Plynlimon just two miles from the source of that other great river, the Severn, sister rivers that take very different courses. The Severn, Britain's longest river, takes a 210-mile passage, heading north-easterly before changing direction to make its way to the Bristol Channel via a historic route that includes Shrewsbury, which it all but makes an island; Ironbridge, the birthplace of the Industrial Revolution; two cathedral cities, Worcester and Gloucester; and in its lower reaches imposing a barrier that greatly contributed to the long isolation of the Forest of Dean as a separate community.

The Wye, a river of great charm, takes a shorter but highly scenic route rarely pursuing a straight course for long, but meandering through Wales and England for 130 miles before mingling its waters with the Severn just below Chepstow. It is a volatile river, responding quickly to rainfall or melting snow in the Welsh hills. The level rising dramatically, 17 feet above normal is not unknown with flooding an inevitable consequence. In the year that this is being written the streets along the riverside at Hereford were under water. As it nears its journey's end the river is subject to the ebb and flow of the tides, although it does not emulate the Severn with a bore. At Chepstow, once a flourishing port and shipbuilding centre, the tidal rise and fall is an astonishing 49 feet. The normal tidal limit extends as far as Bigsweir Bridge, five miles above Tintern where at times sandbags do duty for doormats. Periods of heavy rain combined with spring tides and high winds have in the past contrived to wash through the abbey grounds with water standing four feet deep in the exhibition centre. All this is not new, for the river has a long history of bridges swept away, villages swamped by the flood, cattle drowned, churches under water and even a graveyard robbed of its dead by the swirling waters.

This sketches in the darker side of the river, a dramatic story of death and destruction which has over thousands of years had its part to play in the formation of the landscape that we see and enjoy today. For the most part the river has a more cheerful disposition,

9

gently murmuring through its quieter stretches, singing away over the stony shallows and sometimes rising to a symphony-like crescendo as it forces it way through a course narrowed by the great rocks that lie in its bed. The power of the river is never in doubt whatever the season and you may see the deep, rounded scoops cut into the softer parts of the rock by pebbles carried on the swirling waters, below the bridge at Rhayader or at Penddol Rocks just above Builth Wells.

The river makes its way through a valley that is characterised by rolling hills, often tree-covered, water meadows where fine cattle graze, the bright blossomed orchards of Herefordshire and in deep gorges with towering limestone cliffs. It provides superb fishing not only for wader-clad, supple-wristed, fly fishermen seeking salmon and trout but for herons who are found throughout its length.

Kingfishers seem to be less plentiful but the glimpse of an electric blue flash as one darts straight as an arrow across the river will be counted as a bonus to any day's walking. That rare creature, the otter, is still reputed to be found along the Wye but seeing one is another matter. Apparently more common are the feral mink escapees from fur farms which have become firmly established in the wild. They are highly destructive creatures killing beyond their need for food, and much hunted by river keepers.

The woods provide fine nesting sites for buzzards and their graceful soaring flight may be enjoyed virtually anywhere along the Wye Valley. A much less common bird is the peregrine which has returned to nest at Coldwell Rocks near Yat Rock. Even rarer is the red kite which survives in mid-Wales and may be seen by explorers of the Elan Valley although it has occasionally been reported in Herefordshire. Fallow deer may be seen in the Forest of Dean or the deep bellow of the rutting stag heard in October; foxes, rabbits and badgers are all present as well as a variety of birds. A feature of the walk is the wild flowers that are to be found in some profusion according to season, a rare treat for some walkers accustomed to more intensively farmed areas of the country.

Whilst classed as a low level long distance walk the route does not keep close company with the river throughout the 112 miles between Rhayader and Chepstow. These diversions away from the river, necessitated by the lack of a suitable right of way or to take advantage of the views afforded by higher ground add variety to the journey but the return to the river is always welcome. The terrain is not difficult; true, there are one or two rougher patches but nothing that any walker worth his salt would regard as in any way extreme. The route follows quiet lanes, field paths and ancient tracks, former railway lines, shaded ways cut off from the world contrast with stretches over high, open hill country where the whirr of the tractor gives way to the mewing of buzzard. Some paths may be overgrown in summer when you are obliged to pick your way at risk from nettle and bramble, or an occasional stretch of road walking encountered that may seem a mite overlong.

Amidst the expected there are little unscheduled cameos of delight, the unanticipated surprise view presenting a window on the world though the trees, or the warming pleasure of a foal with its mother coming up to a fence to be admired - little incidents that are entirely individual to the walker and cannot be set down in print. The hill sections whilst steep in places do not go on interminably, the effort amply repaid with splendid views. The highest point on the way, over 1,300 feet, is found on the Builth to Erwood section.

A succession of quiet villages with ancient parish churches, old market towns like Hay and Ross, the long story of Hereford and its cathedral all add a rich harvest of history and heritage to the walk and time should be made to savour their various pleasures.

Clearly we are not the first to travel this way; even the most casual inspection of the map reveals something of those who have gone before. The Romans had a camp high above the Elan Valley and we meet them again as we tread their long straight road as the lost town of Magnis near Hereford is approached. The name of Hereford itself indicates its origins as a military crossing of the river in Saxon times. The Normans came and built a chain of castles, some are but green mounds but others remain to thrill the visitor as at Goodrich and Chepstow which is doubly distinguished by being the first stone castle built in this country. Before all this our forefathers constructed their hill forts and a succession of these are marked on the map throughout the Wye Valley. Earlier still Stone Age man lived in the caves of the Forest of Dean where traces of his fires still remain in King Arthur's Cave high above the river. Here, too, were unearthed bones of fearsome creatures now long extinct, lion, cave bear and mammoths.

And what of the people we can name? Henry V, immortalised by Shakespeare, was born at Monmouth; Llewellyn the Last (the last Welsh-born Prince of Wales) met a violent death near Builth; Owen Glendower is reputed (but disputed) to have died, apparently peacefully, at Monnington-on-Wye. Nell Gwynne, born in humble circumstances, left her native Hereford to become a king's mistress. A gentle cleric who served as curate at Clyro achieved a posthumous fame in the literary world with the publication of his diaries sixty years after his premature death. This we can be sure would have caused him no little surprise, the more so now that the region has acquired the sobriquet Kilvert Country.

There is much more to tell, of the monks who came to find peace at Tintern; of the industry of the lower Wye Valley and the mines of the Forest of Dean; of the drovers with their dogs carefully herding their charges for long miles over the green hills or splashing through the Wye fords. Sad times of plague, happy days of plenty, the bitter days of the Civil War, the building of Offa's Dyke to mark out the frontier with Wales. Then there was the age of romantic travel when the rich came to take the Wye Tour, artists and poets to find subjects for their canvases and inspiration for their verses. One diarist of the day expressed the view that to enjoy Tintern Abbey to the full it was necessary to bring wine, cold meats and spread a table in the ruins, with a harpist to provide suitable background music to the meal.

All this is surely enough to whet the appetite of today's prospective traveller and the rest must unfold as the journey is undertaken and one map is exchanged for the next.

2: *Practical matters*

The Wye Valley Walk has been developed by several local authorities. At its southern end it is maintained and waymarked by the Wye Valley Countryside Service, a merging of resources by the county councils of Gwent, Gloucestershire and Hereford & Worcester. The walk originally ran from Chepstow to Ross-on-Wye; a further 18 miles was added to take the walk upstream to Hereford. In 1989 the route was again extended to carry it on to Hay-on-Wye, thus linking it with the 36-mile route developed by Powys County Council in Wales. The walk currently terminates, or in the case of this book which follows the river downstream begins, at Rhayader.

Future Developments

As this book is being completed, June 1991, Powys County Council is about to appoint a project officer on a short term contract whose initial task will be to make improvements to the existing walk within its area - Hay-on-Wye to Rhayader. Thereafter there are plans to survey and negotiate access agreements with landowners with a view to extending the walk northwards.

Signing, Waymarking and Wayfinding

In Powys signing at road junctions is generally by a stout post bearing the figure of a walker together with a yellow arrow. Some posts bear the legend Wye Valley Walk. Dual language signing is common in Powys and walkers newly arrived from England soon discover that Llwybr Cyhoeddus is not a direction pointer to a hamlet too small to be found on the map but simply announces a public footpath. The permutations continue on Please Close the Gate notices, Royal Mail vans, toilets and so on - a painless and interesting introduction to the Welsh language - pronunciation is another matter! Off-road waymarking is by plastic discs carrying a yellow arrow on a green background.

Downstream from Hay a similar system operates except that the yellow arrows are accompanied by yellow dots usually on brown

13

Wye Valley Walk signing, Erwood

plastic discs. At road junctions stout posts almost invariably carry "Wye Valley Walk" incised into the upright and additional post signing occurs at important off-road junctions. Painted waymarks

14

may also be found in some wooded sections when extra clarification is required.

Waymarking is on the whole excellent but vandalism and the weather may take their toll, old gateposts collapse with age or lose an argument with a farm tractor. There are a few places where the absence of signing may cause moments of doubt, but no-one should expect to follow the walk by total reliance on waymarks. A "look ahead" to the next turn or landmark indicated in the route description or on the map should avoid all but the occasional problem.

Much of the walking is on good, clear paths; this is particularly so from Ross-on-Wye southwards which is in well walked territory. Obstructions do occur, particularly after high winds in the wooded areas, but the Wye Valley Countryside Service, sometimes assisted by conservation volunteers are usually quick to clear the way. There are one or two sections of lesser used paths in Powys that may become overgrown in summer but as the route gains popularity as a long distance walk even this small inconvenience should disappear as more boots tread the way.

The Wye has changed its course over the centuries, and so, too, does the footpath network, being subject to diversions or improvements as alternatives are found. It is impossible for any book or map to keep fully up-to-date with these, but changes are usually accompanied by a footpath diversion notice and more intensive waymarking. Any serious obstruction to the path, unfriendly barbed wire, or vandalism should be reported to the Wye Valley Countryside Service, Hadnock Depot, Mayhill, Monmouth Gwent (0600 3977) or to the Rights of Way Officer, Planning Dept, Powys County Council, County Hall, Llandrindod Wells. LD1 5LG. (0597 826000)

Maps and Compass

The sketch plans in this book are for general guidance only and should be used in conjunction with the appropriate Ordnance Survey Maps which, as well as putting the walker in the context of the landscape as a whole, provide a vast amount of information for those who learn to use them to the full.

The 1:25,000 sheet (two and a half inches to the mile) is the walkers preferred scale providing much detail. Particularly useful is the inclusion of field boundaries, a useful aid in wayfinding. The

Landranger sheets at 1: 50,000 (one and a quarter inches to the mile) may be used and, of course, fewer of these are required. The appropriate map numbers are noted at the beginning of each section but the full set is listed here for easy reference.

It should be noted that some of the maps have overlapping sections and in the case of the 1: 25,000 some of the sheets only accommodate a very small portion of the walk. The comment column indicates where this occurs and walkers who do not already own that particular sheet may elect to rely on the route description and waymarking to bridge the gap to the next sheet.

1: 50,000 Landranger

Sheet	Area
136 Newtown, Llanidloes	Only required if exploring north of Rhayader to source. Does not include all of Elan Valley area.
147 Elan Valley & Builth Wells	Includes Rhayader and the reservoir and extends south to Erwood.
161 Abergavenny & the Black Mountains ⎫⎬⎭	These two sheets overlap but are not quite complete taken separately.
148 Presteigne & Hay-on-Wye	Extends to eastern edge of Hereford.
149 Hereford, Leominster	Again overlapping but required for south of Hereford.
162 Gloucester & Forest of Dean	Ross-on-Wye to Chepstow.

1: 25,000 Pathfinder and earlier series numbers quoted

969	(SN 86/96)	Rhayader	Includes Elan Valley and reservoirs
970	(SO 06/16)	Llandrindod Wells	Only very small section of walk on extreme south-west corner of this sheet.

991	(SN 85/95)	Beulah	Only small section.
992	(SO 05/15)	Builth Wells	Newbridge to a little south of Builth.
1015	(SO 04/14)	Aberedw	On to Erwood and Llanstephan and required later for part of Glasbury to Hay-on-Wye.
1038	(SO 03/13)	Talgarth	Continues to short distance north of Glasbury.
1016	(SO 24/34)	Hay-on-Wye	Extends eastward to Bredwardine and Byford.
1017	(SO 44/54)	Hereford North	
1040	(SO 43/53)	Hereford South	Includes eastern approach to City on to Mordiford & Brockhampton. (tiny eastern section missing - which extends on to sheet 1041 - ie. Fishpools Hill and then How Caple.
1065	(SO 62/72)	Ross-on-Wye East	Covers sections north and south of the town.
1064	(SO 42/52)	Ross-on-Wye West	Ditto. Extends to within 1 mile of Kerne Bridge.

Thereafter OUTDOOR LEISURE MAP No. 14. WYE VALLEY AND FOREST OF DEAN is advised.

North of Rhayader to Plynlimon the relevant 1:25,000 Pathfinder sheets are noted for future reference.

927	(SN 68/78)	Eastern edge of this sheet covers Plynlimon in part including public rights of way to Pen Pumlumon Fawr.
928	(SN 88/98)	Continuation eastwards towards Llangurig and Llanidloes.
948	(SN 87/97)	Llangurig southwards to just north of Rhayader thereafter as listed.

In addition every walker should carry a compass, however infrequent the need to use it may be. There are times when it will solve

17

minor problems of wayfinding when paths are indistinct or have "disappeared" or in woods where more paths appear on the ground than are sometimes shown on maps. Above all it may be absolutely essential for upland navigation.

Transport

The more rural the area, the thinner transport facilities become and in some places buses are limited to once daily or even only once weekly with Sunday services often non-existent. The situation is much better in the lower Wye Valley; for further comments and sources of timetable information please refer to the Useful Information section at the back of the book.

Accommodation

There is a good spread of accommodation in the main centres with a reasonable choice of bed and breakfast to be found in towns like Rhayader, Builth Wells, Hay-on-Wye, Hereford, Ross-on-Wye, Tintern and Chepstow. In between opportunities may be more limited. Please refer to Useful Information section for further detail.

Clothing and Equipment

Experienced walkers can skip this section; they will have already learnt the importance of being suitably clothed. An examination of the equipment pages featured in various magazines would suggest that being fully equipped is expensive; it need not be so.

There are those with good reason who subscribe to the wearing of stout trainers but I believe that for the average walker boots are the answer. They come in a rich variety, and rich you may have to be to pay some of the prices which are asked. Lightweight boots with good sole grips, padded ankle support, sewn-in tongues and removable insoles are ideal for the Wye Valley terrain. The fabric-topped variety provides great comfort and recent advances have brought onto the market, some which are lined with water-resistant material, but these tend to be rather expensive. Some well-known makes, but without the full waterproofing qualities, are available at more modest prices and will do very well for summer walking in dry weather. Occasional wet feet may not matter very much in summer but are to be avoided in winter. An inexpensive range of lightweight leather boots is available and if these are regularly treated with a specialist waterproofing wax they should keep you dry shod. A little shopping around should enable you to buy a pair of both fabric and leather-topped boots for less than the cost of a pair in the upper price range. Manufacturers are constantly bringing out new lines and the perfect lightweight boot for all occasions and with an acceptable price tag may yet appear.

Buying the right socks is just as important as the boot. Look for loop stitch socks with high wool content, taking care to ensure that they are not too constricting around the calf.

When selecting clothing the aim should be to maintain a comfortable body temperature; cotton shirts and wool sweaters provide the answer. In the cooler seasons lightweight tanktops/ bodywarmers are also useful and have the merit of additional pockets.

Denim is not a material favoured by experienced walkers; when wet it tends to cling to the skin with obvious risks in cold weather. Legs may be better clad in shorts in hot weather, but do get acclimatised and use a well filtered sun tan cream. Breeches are one of the most comfortable of walking garments and can be bought in different weights for use according to season.

Headwear should not be neglected. Cold weather, and upland walkers at all seasons, should be equipped with woollen hats. They may look ridiculous in the High Street but are a godsend in the hills, retaining heat and in strong winds excellent protection from earache. Protection from the sun may be necessary; white floppy hats are both cheap and easily tucked into pockets or rucksacks.

That it rains in this country is an undeniable fact despite the long periods of drought and hose pipe bans that have become a more regular feature of recent summers. Wet weather gear can be another pricey item and you may be torn between the higher-priced garments made of material that "breathes" and lesser-priced items that may leave you with that boiled in a bag feeling. Whatever decision you make take care to buy leggings which are flared and zipped to facilitate putting them on over boots, and that anorak tops have sealed seams and stout zips. Wet weather apart, their windproof qualities are invaluable.

All this needs something to carry it in - again the range of rucksacks is considerable with improvements constantly being found. Look for a product with padded shoulder straps, waist belt, quick release fastenings, adequate side pockets which can be used to accommodate a good size water bottle, for instance. Seams should be double stitched and the material as waterproof as you can afford. A bin liner can be a useful aid - it is worth carrying one anyway to protect delicate items like a camera or to ensure that one set of clothing is kept dry. Study the manufacturer's blurb or test reports in the walking magazines and check on its unladen weight. Regular walkers usually have at least two rucksacks - one for day excursions and a larger pack to meet the needs of longer trips. Think carefully what you are likely to need to carry; don't buy too large - you will only be tempted to fill it - and it is you that will have to carry it.

Common Sense Safety Measures

The Wye Valley Walk is a low-level walk but even so it is worth while sticking to the basic rules of walking. Map and compass have already been mentioned but accidents do happen - are you equipped to cope with them? Minor problems can be solved with a first aid kit which should contain plasters, antiseptic, a roll of pressure bandage, aspirin or similar, sun cream, sting relief and insect repellant.

Four items in addition to my compass that live permanently in my rucksack, whatever the season, are a lightweight survival bag, emergency rations, torch and a whistle. Sounds dramatic? It isn't. Can you be sure you will never need them? Picture yourself with a badly sprained ankle on a winter day with the light beginning to fail, or a similar situation in summer three miles from the nearest road and a thunderstorm just about to break?

One last point - be sure to carry adequate liquid refreshment - preferably water lightly flavoured with fruit juice - in high summer dehydration can be a real danger and some stretches of the walk are well away from a refill.

Seasonal Walking

The Wye Valley Walk can be followed throughout the year provided proper consideration is given to the weather and the available hours of daylight. The rapid rise of water levels on the Wye may result in flooding - be prepared to make diversions. Spring has the freshness of the new season with the successive appearance of wild flowers into high summer. Summer has the advantage of more daylight hours and the possibility of longer periods of settled weather, whilst autumn brings in the fine colours which may be enjoyed to the full in the lower Wye Valley looking down to the forest canopy from Yat Rock or the Seven Sisters. Winter walking has its own invigorating pleasures with leafless trees revealing views denied to summer walkers.

A Good Read

There is not much room for reading matter in a backpack other than the essential maps and guides but one book that may prove rewarding is Kilvert's Diary. The Rev Francis Kilvert kept a series of diaries between 1870 and 1879 and presents an interesting picture of the area. He was a great walker, took note of the countryside and recorded his visits to many of the points along the route in the Hay-on-Wye area. An abridged version is published by Penguin. If you are able to read it before starting your journey you may experience an occasional sense of *déjà vu*.

3: Rhayader and the Elan Valley

Rhayader, the northern end of the Wye Valley Walk, is an excellent point at which to start the long journey down the River Wye for it has been accustomed to catering for visitors for centuries. The town, long established in the hill country of mid-wales, was a stopping place for travellers on the coach road to Aberystwyth providing refreshment, accommodation and a change of horses. The tourist information centre is itself situated in a former seventeenth-century inn, a not inconsistent change of use. It has long been a market town and farmers still come to buy and sell sheep, cattle and ponies, now sometimes watched by curious holidaymakers. The market hall, built in 1762, was demolished in 1923 and was replaced at the crossroads by the clock tower. The twelfth-century castle, which stood close to the church is no more; its epitaph found on the map simply records Rhayader Castle (site of) - the cartographer's version of R.I.P.

The once-famed waterfall that gives the town its name, (the waterfall on the Wye) is now somewhat reduced but the river still tumbles excitingly enough beyond the bridge. Accustomed as Rhayader must have become to the comings and goings of travellers, an event of the 1890s must have caused one of the biggest stirs in the town's history since the Rebecca rioters attacked turnpike toll houses. (This was a Welsh phenomenon where the turnpike charges were particularly resented and not just by the poor. Protesters dressed in women's clothing dragged down the gates and destroyed the toll houses over a wide area in the early 1840s.)It was the coming of a workforce, which reached a peak of 5,000 men, to build the now famous reservoirs of the Elan Valley.

The story begins far away in the heart of the industrial Midlands, Birmingham the city of a thousand trades. Public health in the city had become a major concern of the City Fathers, with frequent outbreaks of smallpox and diarrhoea ascribed to the poor quality of the water supply. A source of pure water was desperately needed, and Birmingham, always a pioneer, found the solution with an imaginative engineering concept that fully took into account the

Garreg-ddhu Reservoir, Elan Valley

principle that water finds its own level.

The hills around the Elan Valley provided an enormous collecting ground for the high rainfall that was needed to stock the reservoirs and the head of water had an inbuilt additional continuing cost-saving advantage. The overall distance from the proposed dams to Birmingham's Frankley reservoir is 73 miles. Careful survey and precise engineering work enabled the water to be piped the entire distance without the need for pumping, it being sent on its way via an inverted syphon. A century later a German engineer on holiday in the area read the information board and was sufficiently impressed to murmur in my hearing "very clever". So it was, and far seeing for the supply that was created was sufficient to assuage the city's thirst for the next fifty years.

It was a considerable undertaking with a series of reservoirs and dams to be constructed down the valley. At the northern end Craig Goch Reservoir covers 217 acres with a 120-foot high dam holding back some two thousand million gallons of water. Penygarreg Dam, 417 feet wide with a spectacular curtain of water falling 123 feet, holds one thousand three hundred and twenty million gallons.

23

Carreg-ddhu, bridged and flowing into Caban-coch, added eight thousand million gallons. The addition of the four-mile long Claerwen Dam in 1952 brought the total overall capacity to over twenty-one thousand million gallons.

All these figures immediately bring to mind the emotive phrase "drowned valley" and it is true that farms and larger houses were lost in the flooding of the valley. The recently married poet, Percy Bysshe Shelley, lived in the valley, at Nantgwllt, during the years 1811-12. Whether his verse might have been in his usually romantic vein had he lived to witness the disappearance of the valley is a matter for speculation. His connection with the area is remembered with a stylized bronze at the Elan Valley Visitor Centre, depicting the poet with pages of his notebook set about him.

The great blocks of stone to construct the dams were brought from the Llanelwedd quarries at Builth Wells. Miles of railway had to be built to take men and materials to the construction sites. Clearly there was not sufficient accommodation in the area to take the men engaged on the project and a temporary village was built for them. More permanent buildings, including a school, were provided for the staff that were to remain to oversee the operation of the dams on completion. The logistical support included a notable "first" for the corporation, becoming the first local authority to operate a public house! The daily outflow from the dams is over one hundred million gallons of which three-quarters goes down the pipeline to the Midlands with the remainder flowing into the River Elan and thence to the Wye.

The excellent visitor centre close to the Caban-coch Dam tells the story of the Elan Valley in succinct fashion, taking in Bronze Age man, the Cistercian monks, tenant farming, and the building of the dams, the whole linked by over 4,000 years of sheep farming.

The upheaval of the construction work has gradually faded away, grass grows upon the old railway tracks, the dams and their green-domed control towers have mellowed into the landscape. Thus the flooding of the valleys of the Elan and Claerwen rivers has created a Welsh lake district attracting an increasing number of visitors.

Today Rhayader has become a small holiday resort, a centre for touring the delightful countryside of mid-Wales and yet still within reach of the coast. Its special attractions include fishing, pony trekking - by the day or week and birdwatching with a mix of habitats - waterside, broad-leaved and coniferous woodland, and open hill country. Here the "twitcher" or "birder" may increase his score of "ticks" with sightings of many birds of prey including buzzard, peregrine and the rare red kite. The kite, which had become all but extinct, has been the subject of a long and careful conservation programme involving the RSPB and the Nature Conservancy Council with numbers slowly increasing. Throughout the length of the Wye Valley Walk the call of a day-hunting owl is to be heard. Added to these is a mix of both familiar and less common birds which may encourage those with only a hitherto casual approach of the "I wonder what that bird is" variety to take a closer interest.

This countryside, with its rivers flowing clean and clear, shady woods not eclipsed by the more severe conifer plantations and framed in a setting of rounded hills and rocky outcrops which supports a spread of resident and migratory birds, presents a landscape that is particularly attractive for walkers. In the first section of the Wye Valley Walk all its component features are encountered.

Notes:

Elan Valley Visitor Centre is open during the summer months between 10.00am and 6.00pm.
The Rhayader Museum, East Street, which features various aspects of local history, is open on varying days between Easter and the end of September.

4: Rhayader to Newbridge

DISTANCE:	9¹/₂ miles approx.
DETAIL:	Quiet lanes to the crossing of the River Elan followed by ascent to 1,200 feet giving fine views from open hill country. Lanes and tracks beyond Llanwrthwl offer further views across the Wye Valley.
MAPS:	1:25,000 Pathfinder 969 (SN 86/96): Pathfinder 970 (SO 06/16) small section: Pathfinder 991 very small section: Pathfinder 992 (SO 05/15) 1:50,000 Landranger 147
TOILETS:	Rhayader near cattle market and west of bridge. On route at Llanwrthwl. Car park opposite New Inn at Newbridge - off route.
ACCOMMODATION:	Rhayader. Newbridge. (Motel at Llanwrthwl)
SHOPS:	Rhayader. Newbridge off route east of river.
TOURIST INFORMATION CENTRE:	The Old Swan, junction South Street and West Street, Rhayader. (0597 810591)

From the clock tower in the centre of the town, head along West Street, passing The Old Swan (seventeenth-century) the mellowed-brick Lion Royal Hotel and the sixteenth-century weatherboarded Cwmdauddwr Arms. The bridge over the Wye is soon met and crossed to enter the separate village of Llansantffraed-Cwmdeuddwr. The official route of the Wye Valley Walk starts a little further on but to make an introduction to the river which is to be your companion for the next 112 miles take the first left turn and go down steps into the park.

The pool under the bridge has now been designated a conservation pool with fishing prohibited. Great rocks obstruct the free progress of the river which raises its voice in anger as it pushes

The Wye tumbling through Rhayader

its way through the narrowed channel. However low the water may be, here is the evidence of a wild and noisy river with smooth "basins" deeply cut into the softer parts of the rock by the relentless unforgiving power of the swirling waters. Fish can be seen clearly in the deep, clear pools where the river holds back for a moment before its course widens and it rushes on over the shallows. The Wye at this point is over 650 feet above sea level; by the time it has reached Hay on the border with England it will have dropped over 400 feet - downhill all the way for the river but not for the walker.

This is but the briefest of meetings with the Wye for it must be left to go its own way for the moment. Having inspected the pool, return to the road and continue along Bridge Street for about 50 yards. Turn left taking the narrow lane which passes the sixteenth-century Triangle Inn with the green hills seen ahead.

Follow the steadily rising lane with wild flowers brightening the wayside, seasonally a strong feature of this walk through Wales into

27

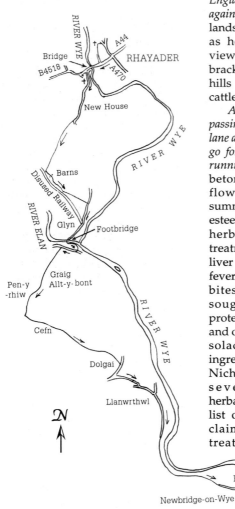

England and back into Wales again. The curtain on a wide landscape is gradually raised as height is gained with views all around to tree-bracken-and grass-covered hills grazed by sheep with cattle in the lower pastures.

About 250 yards after passing New House leave the lane as it swings sharp left and go forward on a rough track running between hedges. Here betony, a reddish-purple flower, flourishes in summer. In times past it was esteemed by practitioners in herbal medicine for the treatment of stomach and liver complaints, to reduce fever and for snake and dog bites. The superstitious sought its powers as a protection against witchcraft and others found a different solace in its use as an ingredient of herbal tobacco. Nicholas Culpepper, the seventeenth-century herbalist, had an extensive list of ailments that were claimed to respond to treatment by betony; in addition to some of those already listed, he recommended its use to stop nose bleeds, ease earache, treat boils - a regular cure all. In the language of flowers it is supposed to indicate surprise - in view of the widespread virtues attributed to it "that figures" as the Americans would say.

The track is followed for half a mile with almost a complete circle of hills making up the horizon; forward to your right are the steep heights above the first of the Elan Dams. When a dismantled railway is reached turn sharp left on the farm track which runs parallel with it. In a few yards the way passes between a pair of barns with the track soon bending to the right. At this point turn sharp left, (do not pass between the abutments of the former railway bridge) to pursue the track south-easterly for 700 yards, with the Cerrig Gwynion quarries seen ahead.

On reaching the metalled lane turn right; in July rosebay willow herb, meadow sweet and birdsfoot trefoil are found along the hedgerow. The lane, little used by traffic, is followed for a quarter of a mile to meet once more with the Wye. A delightful picture it presents as it flows some 60 feet below the lane, ceaselessly chattering away to itself - and to anybody ready to pause and listen. The first of many memorable cameos of the river is partly veiled by the trees but the meeting is brief and the lane swings away to the right to pass between the now unbridged gap in the railway embankment. Beyond, the small scatter of buildings of Glyn is met. Turn immediately left, in front of a barn and pass through a five-barred gate to follow the wide track for 250 yards to reach the River Elan.

The track dips down to the ford but the walker passes dry shod by way of a narrow swaying, swinging, suspension bridge that adds an extra excitement to the walk. What a handsome river the Elan is, tree-lined and rocky-bedded with fine views from the centre of the bridge - here the photographer has to steady himself and wait for the bridge to cease its motion before the shutter can be safely clicked. Rising in Dyfed the river has but a relatively short course to run, just 17 miles, much of that engineered by way of the reservoirs. The harvest of the waters that would once have added further strength to the Wye is gathered in and stored for the domestic and industrial needs of Birmingham. The Elan is not entirely strangled by the tourniquet of the dams that stems the flow and diverts it to a man-made artery, for a steady 29 million gallons a day is released to allow the river to continue on its way sweet and clean.

Once over the bridge turn left through a gate and continue along the path close to the river's edge to the point where the Elan adds its contribution to the water of the Wye. A donation thankfully received, for at this point the Elan tends to look the larger of the two, together they flow on with strength renewed.

Just beyond this marriage of the waters pass through a metal gateway to reach a lane and turn right to follow it for 200 yards. As a house is reached take the fenced path on the left (by a pair of double gates) which climbs steeply for 200 yards to emerge into more open hill country.

The path climbs southwest for half a mile along the western edge of Graig Allt-y-bont. The steadily improving views include Rhayader to the north, almost lost in its farmland setting. There is a wide prospect across the Elan Valley of a patterned landscape of fields rising to give way to the beautifully sculptured and partly wooded hills which enclose the valley. Here as in many other places along the walk the mewing call of a buzzard may be heard. Your attention thus attracted, watch for its easy graceful flight, sailing with the wind on broad wings with rounded tail.

As the path climbs the bracken-covered hillside the broad-leaved woodland on the right gives way to fir plantations. As the plantation falls back the house at Pen-y-rhiw is seen to the right, with a windlass installed to harness some of the power of the wind. Sensible and not obtrusive here, but a whole forest of them would be unthinkable. Pause here to look back once more to the view to the north.

As you draw level with the house the path joins a stony track which should be pursued for a further 200 yards before swinging with it to the south-east as it is joined by a track coming in from the west. All the uphill work has been completed for a while. About 250 yards after the change of direction a gate is reached and a notice announces that you have just passed through the RSPB's Crongafallt Common reserve.

Continue with the track beyond the gate soon to pass through a further metal gateway as you approach the farm buildings of Cefn. What marvellously airy views there are from here! The valley of the Wye opening up ahead to provide a wide perspective of clouds chasing across shapely hills which roll away to infinity, a long view that the camera fails to fully capture.

From Cefn the broad, falling track is followed for just over half a mile, passing through an oak plantation where the trees cling perilously to the

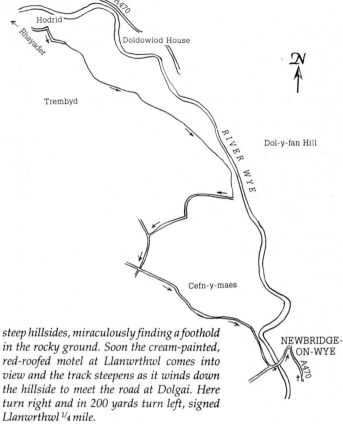

steep hillsides, miraculously finding a foothold in the rocky ground. Soon the cream-painted, red-roofed motel at Llanwrthwl comes into view and the track steepens as it winds down the hillside to meet the road at Dolgai. Here turn right and in 200 yards turn left, signed Llanwrthwl ¼ mile.

At this point the signpost may prompt a little fun for its other arms both point to Elan Village 4¼ miles but in opposite directions. Never mind the logical explanation - get the camera out.

Having resisted the temptation to unravel the mystery of the signing to Elan Village take the road to Llanwrthwl, a small village tucked beneath the hills and not far from the river.

At the village take the lane on the right which passes Saint Gwrtwl's

31

Doldowlod House from the Wye Valley Walk

parish church which is followed through to Mill Bridge with its chapel and large tombstones with the inscriptions easily read from the roadside. Continue with the Wye coming into earshot and ultimately into view through the trees, cooling waters, tantalisingly out of reach, with whitened stones in high contrast with the blue sky faithfully reflected in the river. Soon the lane is passing under the lee of the dark pines of Caegarw with the Wye sparkling below and the hedgerow offering the possibility of an unexpected bon bouche of wild raspberry. The river is soon left behind, is this to be the extent of the friendship - a mere nodding acquaintance with travellers whose paths cross and recross at intervals? Fear not the friendship will blossom in the fullness of time.

A mile and a quarter from Llanwrthwl the hamlet, if that isn't too big a word, of Hodrid is reached, beautifully kept houses under the green slopes of the 1,558-feet high Trembyd. Take the sharp bend to the right and continue with the metalled lane until it comes to an abrupt end at a metal gateway. There are now two miles of excellent walking along a broad grassy *track which terraces the hillside, bracken-clothed slopes to the right and a stone wall on your left enclosing a band of conifers falling down to the valley.*

At last the blindfold of the trees is removed and fine views are presented over the dry stone wall to the handsome Doldowlod House beyond the far bank of the Wye. The stone-built house responds kindly to the sun, enhancing its appearance with Doldowlod beyond the main road providing a green backing. At the north top of the wood the map makes a point of indicating Laundry Cottage and since this lies close to a series of pools the name would appear to have an obvious origin.

James Watt, 1736-1819, whose development of steam power did so much to advance the Industrial Revolution, bought the small farmhouse here as a country retreat from his work in Birmingham, where he was in partnership with Matthew Boulton. Later, in 1827, Watt's son, also James, added to the house, with the original farmhouse being removed some fifty years later as the building was further extended.

A little beyond your viewpoint to Doldowlod the track divides; ignore the right fork which heads off up the hill. When a clump of firs is seen on the hillside to the right it is time to change to the next map if you are using the 1:25,000.

Over the river Dol-y-fan Hill rises strikingly to 1,220 feet, with an acne-like eruption of craggy rocks breaking out on its western face. As the hill comes into view through the trees pass through wooden gateway, continue with the track to reach and continue forward on a metalled lane. Cross a bridge and bend right with the road. From here on unless you have bought the full set of the 1:25,000 which were listed there is a small gap but there should be no problem in completing the walk through to Newbridge. There is rather a long stretch of road walking but there is little traffic and some good views.

The lane rises steadily; in about 700 yards the gated way to Upper Cefncoed is passed on your left. Continue with the road to meet T-junction in 600 yards, here turn left (this should be waymarked) and in 600 yards meet a minor crossroads and turn left.

Now the lane descends with airy views; looking half-right the sharp-nosed Hay Bluff will be seen marking the eastern boundary of the Black Mountains. Soon the little village of Newbridge will be seen across the

33

Wye, not directly on the route unless accommodation has been booked there. From the last crossroads it is a full mile and a quarter to the junction with the B4358 on the western side of the bridge over the Wye.

Walkers travelling on to Builth Wells should now turn right and refer to the next chapter. Those staying overnight in Newbridge or hoping to pick up supplies at the shop and refreshment at the inn should turn left and once over the bridge take the path on the right that makes a short cut to the village. The longer route by the road passes Mid Wales House, an old drovers' inn, more of this in the next chapter.

5: Newbridge-on-Wye to Builth Wells

DISTANCE:	7 miles approx.
DETAIL:	A modest amount of road walking with field and woodland paths leading on to 4 miles of particularly fine riverside scenery.
MAPS:	1:25,000 Pathfinder 992 (SO 05/15) 1:50,000 Landranger 147.
TOILETS:	Newbridge village car park and Builth Wells car park.
ACCOMMODATION:	Newbridge. Builth Wells.
SHOPS:	Newbridge (limited). Builth Wells.
TOURIST INFORMATION:	Groe car park (by river) Builth Wells. (0982 553307).

Walkers not actually stopping over in Newbridge may find it worth while to make a small diversion to the Wye bridge, a modern, functional product of the twentieth century, the latest in a series of bridges and certainly not the one that gave the village its name which may well date back to the fourteenth century. The inscription that recorded the opening of its predecessor in 1911 states that it "replaces a timber bridge of great antiquity". It has long been a crossing place, and with the shallow waters often only ankle deep, the Romans are thought to have made use of it. It was here that the drovers brought their charges on the way to the English markets or for fattening in richer pastures. If you look over the bridge on the downstream side the old ford can be clearly seen. Here the bank dips down to the water with the drove way still visible on the east bank. The clump of Scots Pine by the river may be more than decorative planting for these trees were often planted to signal the availability of accommodation and refreshment for the drovers.

Here as at Erwood further downstream you may picture the clangour of the drove with men and dogs herding the long lines of cattle, perhaps several hundred strong. Certainly the onward trek would be halted here while the cattle drank their fill, with those at the back of the long line scenting water anxious to join their fellows in the cooling river.

There is no certainty about the origin of the old drove ways but the network out of Wales seems to have been well established 800 years ago. At the peak thousands of cattle were moved through mid-Wales via places like Rhayader, Newbridge, Builth, Erwood and Clyro. Not that Wales was the only cattle droving country; movement was widespread. North Yorkshire's Hambleton Road, an ancient green lane, was used by drovers bringing cattle south from Scotland for fattening and the London markets from the fourteenth century and probably much earlier. Cattle move slowly and the journey would have been a long one with perhaps 10 or 12 miles the sum total of a day's progress.

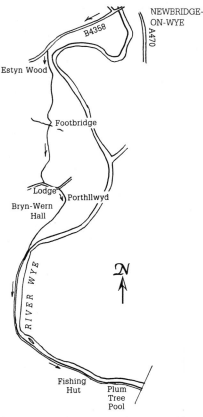

Eating on the hoof is a modern expression suggesting a quickly grabbed lunch - but cattle and sheep would be seizing every opportunity for a bite from the hedgerows and verges. The passage over the open hillsides would have kept men and their dogs even busier keeping the herd together and moving on. It may be imagined that there was a sigh of relief when they were able to funnel their charges into the lanes with their confining hedges.

Frequent overnight stopping places would be required where

the stock could be kept in relative safety and refreshment found for the drover and his men. Many of the older inns that survive today catering for the motoring tourist have a history of attending upon the needs of the drovers and this may well have been the main reason for their existence. One such inn was Mid-Wales House, a sixteenth-century inn, on the road just beyond the east bank of the Wye at Newbridge. Today it is following a new career as a Welsh craft centre but it retains much of its former character. The original oak timbers are still to be seen, now so toughened with age that it has become impossible to drive in a nail.

The coming of the turnpike system added to the cost of droving - a table of tolls displayed at the Singleton Open Air Museum in Sussex includes in its tariff "For every score of Oxen, Cows or Neat Cattle the sume of tenpence". Calves, sheep, lambs or swine were charged at half this rate. Thus the drovers took care to avoid the bridges and turnpikes, keeping to the greenways wherever possible. The hard metalled roads took their own toll on the hooves of animals more used to softer ways and cattle had to be shod so it was not only innkeepers that benefited from the passing trade.

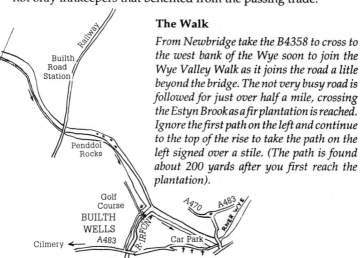

The Walk

From Newbridge take the B4358 to cross to the west bank of the Wye soon to join the Wye Valley Walk as it joins the road a litle beyond the bridge. The not very busy road is followed for just over half a mile, crossing the Estyn Brook as a fir plantation is reached. Ignore the first path on the left and continue to the top of the rise to take the path on the left signed over a stile. (The path is found about 200 yards after you first reach the plantation).

The track makes a sometimes indistinct, twisting, but waymarked passage southwards for a quarter of a mile through Estyn Wood. The Wye may be heard deep below as it loops under the eastern edge of the wood, but it will be some time yet before the walker joins company with it. The way is soggy in places as a small stream dribbles its way through the wood.

Leave the wood by a stile and go forward up the hillside with views soon opening up to the left including the spire of Newbridge church consecrated in 1883 having been built at the personal cost of Mr George Venables for £4,600. Exit from the field having taken a diagonal course to the opposite corner and pass through a metal gateway. Continue with the boundary fence to your right. At the end of a short field pass through a further metal gateway and continue still with the boundary fence to your right.

At the end of the field pass through a wooden gateway and head diagonally left to the corner of the field where you take the narrow path to your right. After a few yards swing left down to a stream to cross the metal footbridge over the Hirnant. Continue forward, still maintaining a generally southerly direction, crossing a reedy field to reach and pass through a metal gateway. Continue onward ignoring the track which swings to the left and go forward to a line of trees to exit at the top of field. (At the time of writing this the exit is guarded by strands of wire, the top one being of barbed wire). Now head diagonally left to the top corner of the field - the path itself may not be visible - and bear left to follow the hedgeline on your right. At the end of this short field pass through an old gateway and maintain direction, but this time with the boundary fence on your left.

At the end of this long field, a meadow with wild flowers as I write, exit by a metal gate. Continue forward with trees to your right to join farm track and leave by a metal gateway to join a lane by the grounds of Bryn-Wern Hall. Here turn left and follow the lane for about 250 yards passing the lodge. Take the waymarked farm road (Porthllwyd), passing through the farmyard, leaving by metal gates on the left. Go forward on a broad track, in a few yards passing through a further gateway with the fenced track continuing for a hundred yards.

Pass through a gateway and immediately through another into the next field and head across at a slight angle a little to the north of a small clump of firs. Pass through a gateway and turn right to exit by a gate and head diagonally right towards woods and double posts of a former gateway seen clearly ahead.

Swing left as waymarked on the posts and cross a plank bridge over a *stream and in a few paces cross a small stile. Mount steps to reach and pass a bungalow to reach the river which is now followed downstream to Builth although some further directions are still required.*

From the bungalow take the narrow path under the trees and when this divides take the upper path which runs parallel with the river. A stile is crossed with the path continuing into a plantation with a fence to your right and the river well below. Presently a further stile is reached and crossed with the narrow path gradually descending through the darkness of the plantation towards the river. A currently unbridged stream and a stile is crossed. From here on the path is never far from the water's edge, following the field and wooded paths, with conifer plantations rising steeply up the slopes which close in from the right.

Here the river shows its varying moods, happy to display its more tranquil side as it offers almost unbroken mirror images in the stilled waters placed under restraint by the weirs. But its restless nature cannot be contained for long and once released it dashes on its way in a joyous turmoil.

After about a mile and a quarter a handsome bungalow will be seen at the top of a slope with steps leading down to a fishing hut - a magnificent location. From the stile which takes the walker in front of the hut there is one of the most beautifully peaceful stretches of the river. Otters are known to frequent this stretch with feral mink in competition. These escapees from fur farms have become a menace on inland waters destroying more fish than they consume. I was told that some 22 mink had been killed within a few months.

From the fishing hut continue on a broad track and at the top of the rise when the track swings to the right, continue forward to resume the field paths alongside the river. A succession of fields are crossed, then more broad-leaved woodland as the railway bridge is approached. Its strictly utilitarian design is considerably enhanced by its reflection in the river.

From the bridge continue on the narrow path to emerge into the open in about half a mile. Here the river roars away as it is forced to make its way in a great torrent through the narrowed gap formed by Penddol Rocks. Again the relentless surge has sent swirling pebbles to scour out bowls in the rock. It is an entirely delightful place with the trees enclosing the river upstream and shoals of small fish gathering in the quieter places under the rocks.

It is a favoured spot for birds - sitting here one sunny morning two herons came and went several times and a grey wagtail with its bright yellow underside and quivering tail darted back and forth. Better still, a brilliantly dressed kingfisher in blue and orange sat upon a rock less than 20 feet away. Here was a rare chance to see this most exciting bird properly, not the usual brief luminescent flash of colour half-seen as it darts along the river banks - one of the few kingfishers I have seen along the Wye although found in much greater numbers along its sister river, the Severn.

Continue downstream for half a mile until the River Irfon, a substantial tributary of the Wye bars your way. Here again at the meeting of the waters two fishermen awaited their chance - one a man with a rod and line, the other a long-necked heron.

Turn sharp right to leave the field by a gateway to reach the road on the outskirts of Builth. Turn left and in a few yards left again to cross the Rhosferig suspension bridge erected in 1984 to replace an earlier bridge which had done duty for 145 years. Once over the bridge turn left to follow the tarmac path through the park and on reaching the Wye continue with the path for half a mile to reach the Wye Bridge at Builth.

6: Builth Wells (Llanfair-ym-muallt)

Builth Wells is a pleasant town with something of the atmosphere of the Victorian era and essentially Welsh in character. Its buildings are a mix of brick and stone, slate-roofed, and looked over by the green hill of the Garth. It has not yet been overtaken by the plethora of universal shop facias which makes one High Street rather too much like the next. There are still little cobbled alleyways like the one that runs past the Drovers' Tea Rooms and the antique shop "Past and Present" sums up the town's ambience. The many hotels and inns represent its days as a spa town, a crossing place on the long droving trail and today's resort as a touring and holiday centre for mid-Wales.

The town is graced by the Wye tumbling over the bedrock creating a succession of lacy frills beyond the six-arched bridge where ever hopeful fishermen cast their lines. The bridge is seen at its most picturesque in the evening light as the sun bathes it and the river in a delicate pink. On the east bank of the river at Llanelwedd the Royal Welsh Showground draws large numbers of farmers and visitors to the show held towards the end of July. Beyond lie the quarries advancing up the hillside like a carefully sliced layer cake. It was from these quarries that much of the stone was cut to build the Elan dams. A case of coals to Newcastle, you might have thought when you look at the rocky nature of the hills surrounding the Elan Valley but the stone cut there proved unsuitable.

The Wells part of the name came rather late in the town's history. Interpretations of earlier versions of the name include "mound of the Silures", and "wild ox of the mountain". This connection will be noted in the handsome bull depicted on the plaque on the market hall of 1877 which now houses the Wyeside Art Centre.

Builth has seen its time of troubles, flood and fire adding to the miseries of the long periods of conflict reflected in the turbulent pages of Welsh history. Before the use of less combustible materials towns and villages were very susceptible to the risks of fire with a rapid spread of the blaze from one building to the next. Builth was no exception and the town was ravaged by serious fires on at least three occasions.

Centre of the strife was the castle around which the town developed. All that remains now is a high, steeply sloped and ditched green mound but enough to confirm that here once stood a very substantial fortification. Like so many others of its kind it started as a simple motte and bailey. The motte is an earth mound on which the Normans placed a timber tower, which was protected by an outer defence of a fenced bank and ditch. The remains of these early Norman castles are common features of much of the country and are particularly plentiful along the borders of England and Wales. The sites of a number of these motte and baileys were to serve as more secure fortifications with their development as stone castles. One such was Builth, a strong link in the chain of castles built at the behest of Edward I in his determination to secure Wales as part of his kingdom. Stone or not, Builth is not one of Edward's castles that have survived, its masonry being removed for building purposes within the town during the sixteenth century. Its importance was such that it is often mentioned in the same listings as such famous survivors as Caernarvon and Harlech. Edward would surely grieve to see its present state, with thistle and briar today providing the only defence against intruders. From the mound a view may be had of the town and the surrounding countryside, the Wye following an uncharacteristically straight course upstream from the bridge, the nearer landscape dominated by the sharp-cut quarries to the east of the river and the steep slopes of the 922-foot high Garth to the south.

Builth Castle cannot be mentioned without reference to the last Welsh born Prince of Wales, Llywelyn ap Gruffydd, often referred to as Llywelyn the Last. His story is a complicated one, with periods of conflict and uneasy peace, as he sought to retain his authority in Wales. Llywelyn captured Builth Castle in 1260, apparently with the collusion of some of its defenders. Seven years later Llywelyn was formally recognised as Prince of Wales by Henry III but this was by no means the end of the turmoil which characterised his life. The succession to the throne of Edward brought further problems with the reluctance of Llywelyn to perform the oath of loyalty. Llywelyn was also in periodic conflict with other Welsh leaders, including his brother Davydd. By 1276 there was open war between the forces of Edward, under the command of Roger Mortimer, and

Llewelyn and his supporters. It was a war of attrition with the Welsh taking advantage of the terrain but in the end Llewelyn was obliged to formally acknowledge Edward's sovereignty. Edward appears to have acted generously in his treatment of Llewelyn with some years of peace ensuing, not an entirely happy time for within a short period of his marriage at Worcester cathedral in 1278 he was to lose his wife, Eleanor Montfort, in childbirth. Edward's reign in Wales was not popular, it seems clear that his administrators had neither the sense nor the grace to make use of the velvet glove in ruling the country. The voices of discontent inevitably were channelled in Llewelyn's direction. It is not hard to see that appeals for help were unlikely to go unanswered and in the spring of 1282 he and his brother were again in revolt with the uprising spreading across the principality.

Edward was not the man to give way to force of arms and he personally headed the army that he determined should once and for all put an end to insurrection. Llewelyn was not without his successes but he was faced by larger forces; he probably realised that in the end he could not win. As winter advanced Edward offered harsh terms of surrender, which seems to have in effect meant exile from Wales with a grant of lands in England. This could hardly have been expected to have met with an acceptance by a man of Llewelyn's calibre and maybe he hoped that by prolonging the issue he might achieve a more favourable solution. Perhaps with that in mind, he made a move to leave the mountains of Snowdonia which were becoming increasingly hazardous for him as the snows of winter were signalled and Edward's grip on the coast and the passes tightened. By mid-December Llewelyn was dead.

The story of his death and the events leading up to it are hedged about with legend. In the apparent belief that an ambush had been laid for him he hid on the rocky hillside above Aberedw, where his hideout is still known today as Llewelyn's cave. Echoes of Robert the Bruce you may think, but without the same outcome. He attempted to take refuge in Builth Castle but was refused sanctuary. Llewelyn, on his way to rejoin a group of his men engaged in a minor battle, was killed by the enemy but only recognised after his death. His head was struck off and despatched to London, presumably as proof of his death, where it was placed on a spike at the Tower of London.

Llywelyn's memorial is found at Cilmery, a village west of Builth, with a dual dedication in Welsh and English. It stands on a green mound with a whitewashed cottage and oak tree behind. A sharp splinter of Welsh stone points an accusatory finger to the sky, with the simple inscription:

Near this spot was killed our Prince Llywelyn 1282.

Now seven centuries later no matter from whence we come, all can acknowledge the bravery of a doughty fighter and champion of independence. Locally it is believed that the Welsh bowmen who defended Llywelyn were also cut down and take their long final rest in the graveyard of Llanynis church.

Builth had other troubles over and above fire, flood and years of conflict and it must seem in retrospect that the four horsemen of the Apocalypse had ridden this way on more than one occasion. The little stream to the west of the town, the Nant yr Arian (the brook of silver), as it was renamed, recalls the dreaded days of the plague. This was once one of the town's boundaries, and it was to this "no man's land" that the farmers brought supplies to be collected by the surviving townsfolk. Payment was left in the brook on the premise that the waters would wash away the infection, a tragic story that we shall see repeated elsewhere as our journey continues down the Wye Valley.

The therapeutic properties of water were to form another, but happier chapter in the life of Builth with its development as a spa town as the fashion for the social and medical benefits of "taking the waters" spread. Unlike the leading spa towns of Bath, Buxton and Cheltenham, there is little in the town to remind the visitor of those days although Park Wells will be seen on the map just a little to the north-west. Park Wells was saline in character, with the sulphur content of Glanne Wells perhaps owing something to the volcanic origins of Llanelwedd Rocks.

St Mary's Church, as might be expected, makes its own contribution to the history of the town. John Wesley, mainspring of Methodism, came here on a number of occasions during the course of his long missionary journeys. So great were the crowds clamouring

The memorial to Llywelyn, the last Welsh born Prince of Wales, Cilmery

to hear him that he had to preach in the churchyard. Many of his congregation spoke only Welsh and he had need of the services of an interpreter to convey his message of salvation.

Just inside the church porch lies the much-worn effigy of John Lloid, a Sheriff and Justice of the Peace in Elizabethan times. Close by is a slate tablet commemorating another member of the Lloid family; the inscription is worth recording:

Jane, daughter of John Will, Esq., wife to Marmaduke Lloid Esq.,
deceased 26th Feb. 1696 aged 76.
She's entered into Glory, Free from strife,
Gracious mother and a careful wife,

45

> *Five pious children did survive her here,*
> *To imitate here until they shall appeare,*
> *Since entered into glory, one of five,*
> *God grant long life to them that do survive*

The church, which like the town has seen a succession of rebuildings, the last in 1870, has one or two modern decorative features of interest. These include The Lord's prayer, carefully crafted in lace by E.Mauden Morson in 1960. At the west end of the church is a stained glass window presented by George Sace to "commemorate the coming of peace May 8th 1945 and in thanksgiving for many blessings". Decorative as well as useful is the fine set of hand-embroidered kneelers of varying designs but with the Prince of Wales' feathers prominent. I rather think Llywelyn would have liked that, even though their adoption and the motto Ich Dien, (I serve) was not his but that of Edward, the Black Prince, in the following century.

7: Builth Wells to Erwood

DISTANCE:	6¹/₂ miles to Erwood Bridge - 7 to village.
DETAIL:	Lanes and old tracks lead to a high passage over open hill country with wide views.
MAPS:	1:25,000 Pathfinder 992 (SO 05/15)
	SO 04/14 (Pathfinder 1015)
	1:50,000 Landranger 147
TOILETS:	Builth Wells and Erwood Village.
ACCOMMODATION:	Builth Wells. Erwood.
SHOPS:	Builth Wells - note refreshments at Erwood Old Station - east of bridge.
TOURIST INFORMATION:	Groe car park, Builth Wells. LD2 3BL (0982 553307)

From the riverside car park (Groe Park) go forward to the road and turn left towards the bridge. Now bear right and head down Castle Street, passing the Wyeside Arts Centre on your left. Continue with the road for about 200 yards to bear right on the lane which passes Old Castle House. The road curves round Castle Mound, (perhaps with the ghost of Llywelyn still demanding sanctuary), and is followed until the Newry Road is reached where you turn left. The road is followed for nearly a mile before any further direction is needed, first crossing a stream by a former mill, and then Newry Farm.

Beyond Newry Farm the road gradually narrows, and after Sunnybank rises steadily. At the top of the rise, the road swings to the right; ignore this and continue forward with the lane losing a little height. In season the hedgerow here is thick with foxglove, a long guard of honour decked out in light purple. Forward and half-right is seen the 1,539-feet high Pant-y-llyn Hill.

The lane makes a sharp curve to the right and falls sharply with the Duhonw, a cool, clear stream running between shady banks, announcing its presence before it can be seen. Cross by a footbridge and continue to pass a white house, the metalled track having come to an end. The path now climbs, soon widening into a deep, hollow way, a track which clearly has

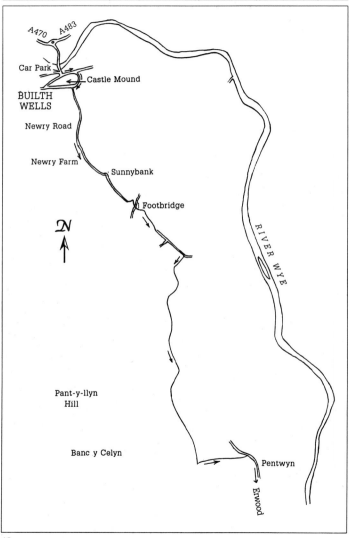

The Wye Valley south from Cefn near Llanwrthwl

*Evening calm on a quiet section of the Wye
near Builth Wells*

been used for centuries, deeply cut between its banks, comfortable to walk, but shut off from the world with thick hedges on either side of the hollow. Further uphill the bedrock protrudes and it is clear that when it rains this track will be very wet underfoot.

At the top of the rise a minor road is met; go forward, climbing steeply with glimpses of a widening landscape. About 300 yards after joining the lane a crossing lane is met, turn right with this, climbing again. At the bend in the track there are good views, with a distant prospect of Builth Wells. The town is on the west bank of the river, and when the Royal Welsh Show is imminent its black slate roofs are in high contrast with the acres of white canvas beyond the river.

Continue with the lane and in a short distance as it swings to the right, leave it to go forward through a metal gateway, still climbing with improving views of the green Radnorshire hills rising beyond the Wye. In 200 yards swing sharp right with the track. In a further 200 yards pass through a metal gateway as the track turns half-left, with Pant-y-llyn seen half-right, taking its name from the small lake lying beneath its western slopes. The walker is now in the open hill country that never fails to produce a feeling of freedom; unhedged, unhindered with the cares of the world falling away like magic.

In about 60 yards bear left with the track, following the fence line on your left. The route runs across the eastern flanks of the twin summits of Pant-y-llyn and Banc y Celyn - at 1,549 feet the senior of the two by a mere 10 feet. The hills are covered in bracken and short grass, a countryside dedicated to sheep for thousands of years.

As the way levels out again a metal gateway is seen ahead; pass through this and continue your southward direction following the path close to remains of a boundary fence on an earth bank and stone wall, and crossing a (usually) dried up stream. Exit by a gate after about a quarter of a mile and go forward a short way to a gateway seen ahead (not the one on the left). Continue southwards, still through the moorland country, following the fading fence line with ancient posts, like rotting teeth, rising out of an earth bank.

In 300 yards pass through a further waymarked metal gateway and continue southwards for well over half a mile on a wide clear track through bracken-covered moorland. The track passes close to a spring, rising then dipping into the clefts worn by streams. Ignore the path which is seen to run diagonally left and continue to the boundary fence where a waymark

The track over the moorland above Alltmawr

directs you eastwards steeply downhill to reach a metal gateway in 600 yards.

As you descend the hillside there are views to the little village of Aberedw, site of yet another castle. Above the village is the cave in which Llywelyn the Last is said to have hidden on the night before his death in December 1282.

Once through the gateway follow a grassy way which soon runs into a metalled track, continue downhill to meet a lane and turn right. This lane is now followed for 1¼ miles, a high level way parallel with the A470 with fine views to the wild hillside of the Aberedw Rocks opposite. Walkers heading south have the best of it for there is no climbing and as progress is made there is a superb aerial prospect that includes the Wye in one of its straighter stretches as it heads for Erwood Bridge.

After about a mile the lane makes a steep descent. A little after passing New House, the road takes a sharp turn to the left. At this point take the track on the right which crosses the Fernant stream by a footbridge. Once over the stream take the track which bears slightly to the left, and in about 100 yards pass through a metal gateway and maintain your direction on the track which is indistinct in places. This leads on to yet another metal

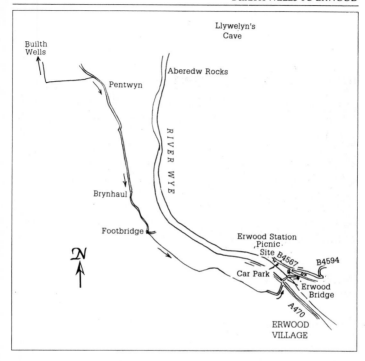

gateway; beyond this the path soon divides, take the lower path through bracken, ie. the left one, and continue with a hedge to your left. The path traverses the hillside and about half a mile after leaving the road the path divides sharply. Watch out for the waymark and take the gully which runs steeply downhill half-left. It soon opens out to a broad track rising again to meet the road in about 600 yards. Turn left with the road which meets the A470 in about a quarter of a mile.

Those continuing should go forward over Erwood Bridge, where refreshment may be found at the craft centre housed in the building that was once Erwood's railway station. Those with accommodation arranged in the village should turn right along the A470 and follow it for about half a mile.

8: Erwood to Glasbury

DISTANCE:	9 miles approx from Erwood Bridge, $9^{1}/_{2}$ approx from Erwood Village.
DETAIL:	Level walking with a good wild flower stretch, views of Black Mountains but some paths may be overgrown in summer.
MAPS:	1:25,000 SO 04/14 (Pathfinder 1015) and Pathfinder 1038 (SO 03/13)
	1:50,000 Landranger 161
ACCOMMODATION:	Erwood Village, Glasbury.
SHOPS:	Glasbury. Refreshments at Erwood Old Station.
TOILETS:	Erwood and Glasbury
TOURIST INFORMATION CENTRE:	Groe car park, Builth Wells. Powys. LD2 3BL (0982 553307)

Walkers heading downstream will not have ventured as far as Erwood Village unless arranging to stay overnight. The village, which has a fine view over the river to the shapely hill of Twyn-y-Garth, has an unexpected association with the sophisticated humour of *Punch* magazine. The sign on the Erwood Inn depicts Henry Mayhew and confides that: "Henry Mayhew resided here in the mid-nineteenth century, his works led to the founding of Punch",

The information presented on the sign is discreet for it has been suggested that his presence in Erwood was not unconnected with a desire to evade some pressing financial commitments. Henry was the son of a London lawyer, his education was entrusted to Westminster School, famed, among other things, for its Shrove Tuesday pancake scramble when the boy who emerges from the scrum with the largest portion wins a guinea. How Henry fared on these occasions does not seem to have been reported but during this period he ran away to sea. On his return he took up law studies and

The Erwood Inn remembers Henry Mayhew, founder of Punch

was articled to his father but writing appealed more than writs and at the age of nineteen he started a weekly magazine. His literary works include *The Wandering Minstrel*, a light-hearted play, and his famous *London Labour and London Poor*, a vivid social indictment, but it is his inspiration that led to the founding of *Punch* for which he is perhaps best remembered. To adapt a phrase of Dr Johnson's "when a man is besieged by his creditors it concentrates his mind wonderfully".

The name Erwood indicates a ford, and the crossing of the river was used by drovers moving cattle to the English markets.

To return to the Wye Valley Walk route take the A470 north-west for just over half a mile. The hedge which borders the road on the right is a good example of a mixed hedgerow with a number of varieties of trees making an attractive as well as an efficient hedge. Hawthorn, oak, beech, ash, elder, hazel, with dog rose and bramble adding flower and fruit.

Turn right to cross Erwood Bridge, a joint enterprise in 1967 between Brecon and Radnor county councils. Both authorities have now vanished, incorporated into the far larger new county of Powys. As with most of the Wye bridges this is an excellent place to pause and enjoy the river views. The hard bed of the river is seen here to perfection when the low summer levels reveal the great shelf of rock, almost a pavement with a narrower, deeper section through which the river forces its way with some turbulence. Downstream the water is fractionally smoother. One can only speculate on the problems the drovers must have encountered in urging their charges across the river. It could never have been an easy task at the best of times and it must have been a nightmare with the river in spate. The cowboys of the Wild West could no doubt have learnt much from the Welsh drovers of old.

At the eastern end of the bridge and below its present level is the old toll house where the turnpike keeper both lived and followed his occupation. They were generally reckoned to have a good job; not only were they provided with a house, they were better paid than many of their fellows "to keep them honest" for clearly there were opportunities for diverting some of the tolls for their own benefit. Not that it was all honey - when the turnpike gates were torn down by a howling mob the keeper and his family could do little but take cover, and trust that the bolts on the door would withstand the hammering of the rioters without. We can imagine them - a frightened family - the wife gathering the children into the comfort of her arms and her husband reinforcing doors and windows with their furniture.

Once over the bridge continue to pass under the former railway bridge and turn left along the road signed to picnic site 300 yards. The familiar path sign with yellow arrow and a little man walking swiftly, but noticeably without a pack on his back, also points the way. Refreshments are available at the former railway station which also houses an arts and crafts centre. The proprietors are well used to catering for walkers returning from the hills and a pot of their excellent tea has revived many a tired walker. The centre is open from 10.00am-6.00pm in summer and to dusk in winter.

The line closed in 1962 and the track has been converted into a metalled

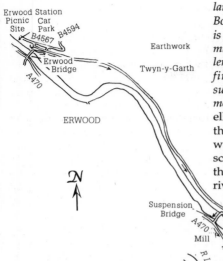

Erwood Station
Picnic Car
Site Park
B4567 B4594
Erwood
Bridge
A470
ERWOOD

Earthwork

Twyn-y-Garth

N

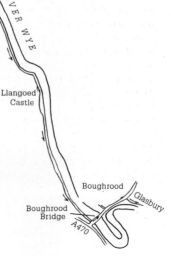

Llanstephan

Suspension
Bridge
A470
Mill

RIVER WYE

Llangoed
Castle

Boughrood

Glasbury

Boughrood
Bridge
A470

lane. Turn left on this signed
*Boughrood 4 miles. The road
is followed for just over 2¼
miles; if the prospect of this
length of road walking is at
first sight unappealing,
suspend judgement for the
moment.* The railway traveller, happy to relax and let
the train take the strain,
would have enjoyed a
scenic route as he, or rather
the train, steamed along the
river valley. One cannot but
pause to lament the lost glory of
these branch lines which, like many
of the canals which they replaced,
wove their way through so many
miles of quite outstanding countryside.

This is a quiet lane affording
good views, allowing a good pace
to get you started on your way and
the bonus of a very fine collection of
wild flowers. The flora, relics of the
undisturbed borders of the track,
has been allowed to flourish by the
highway authority and is now a
designated nature reserve. The
contents of this treasure chest will

55

*Llanstephan suspension bridge, just room for a car and a thin walker
but a tight squeeze with a big rucksack!*

vary according to season, but a quick inventory as we followed the
road in late June included digitalis - (the foxglove - poisonous but
used as a heart drug), field poppy, ox-eye daisy, dog roses, vetch,

56

wall pennywort - (the shape of the leaves gives it its name), herb robert, tufted vetch, meadow sweet, pink campion, buttercup, rose-bay willow-herb, honeysuckle, rock rose, clover, speedwell - surely the walker's choice - species of *Umbelliferae*, and as honesty demands, a good few more with uncertain identification.

After a short distance a fine view opens up to the steep and shapely Twyn y Garth, its 1,066-feet summit crowned with ancient earthworks. About a mile and a quarter after joining the road the route crosses the deep wooded gorge of a stream tumbling down the hillside from Craig Pwll-du, which translates as Black Rock Pool. Sounds interesting; another earthwork and waterfall are also indicated. The map shows a path running through the woods from Llanstephan which might be worth sampling.

From the crossing of the gorge the music of the Wye is again heard, if the water itself is only briefly glimpsed. When the A470 is signed off to the right, turn right over the old railway bridge and in a quarter of a mile reach the fine suspension bridge over the Wye, a bonny bouncing bridge built in 1922, again providing a good prospect of the river, broad and shallow, tumbling over rapids, eager to be on its way, and with a view to the flat-topped Black Mountains. Swifts and swallows find this a good hunting ground, swooping low over the water. Traffic is restricted, with a weight limit of two tons on four wheels, only one vehicle at a time. There is scarcely room for a pedestrian who, if he finds himself sharing the crossing with a car, has to press close to the sides and have a care that he is not grazed by a wing mirror. Bulging rucksacks could be a potential hazard.

Once over the bridge turn left and follow the A470 for 250 yards. Just after passing the handsome mill on your right take the path on the left, heading along the boundary fence above the deeply incised course of Sgithwen Brook to reach the river bank in a hundred yards. Now turn right, downstream, to follow the Wye for two and a half miles. The walk is mostly along field edges with a succession of stiles and gates to be negotiated. Some fine beech trees edge the river which at times lies a full 40 feet below the bank top. Here the river changes mood quickly. Sometimes quieter, deeper, more thoughtful, the flow still enough to reflect the trees that line the banks, before hurrying on again with a rush of white water over little rapids.

About a mile and a quarter down stream from Llanstephan Bridge a handsome building is seen away to your right. This is marked on some maps as Llangoed Castle. The original castle dates back to 1632 but was rebuilt by Clough Williams-Ellis, rather better known for his famous Italian-style village at Portmeirion. The castle is now an hotel, the Llangoed Hall. Along the riverside near here is a clump of fine old sweet chestnuts with crinkled bark, rather like the lattice work found on those superior meat pies with polished crusts.

The path pulls away from the river for a while to pass round a thick clump of trees which conceals a small graveyard within which are memorials to several people from Llangoed Castle. It is a dark and brooding place heavily shadowed by the trees. No wonder there are murmurings of strange stories to be heard locally.

The path returns to the river bank and in a quarter of a mile joins a pleasantly shaded metalled lane which leads from the treatment works of Welsh Water. Continue with the track, passing the handsome stone bungalow of The Shrubbery to reach the road in just over half a mile.

At the road turn left to cross Boughrood Bridge, with a view downstream to the Black Mountains just visible over the trees. Make your way through the village passing the Boat Inn and post office. About a quarter of a mile from the bridge take the path signed off on the right. A narrow way leads down to the riverside, to follow an even narrower, slightly overgrown, in places soggy, but waymarked path. After a short distance the path climbs to the upper bank by a stepped path and continues downstream offering a series of intermittent snapshots of the river through the trees which may include a heron as part of the scene.

About 600 yards after leaving the road, pass through a metal gateway, emerging from the trees to follow the hedge line which is to your left, with views opening up to the Black Mountains. Maintain an easterly direction along field edges to reach a metal gateway which gives access to a broad track which is reached in about quarter of a mile. Pursue this track for 500 yards to reach the road at Boughrood Brest.

Turn right to follow the road, the B4350, for 400 yards to a road junction with a large oak tree and sign which announces "Glangwye". There is also a Wye Valley Walk post.

Take the lane to Glangwye which leads down to the farm and continues as a rough track between hedges. This section is not very good walking and is only redeemed by the fine views of the Black Mountains with the sun playing its age-old game of chasing shadows across the hills.

A single cottage, Applebury, is passed and in 200 yards the track

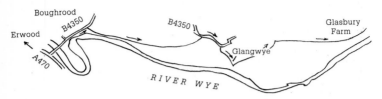

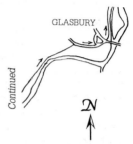

swings to the right; keep with it. Although writ large upon the map the track peters out after a while but maintain your direction, passing through a metal gateway to follow the field edge with a hedge to your left. At the end of the field, pass through a further metal gateway and continue on an indistinct path, again with a hedge to your left, and passing through a small clump of ash trees. The way does not improve although it is obvious it was once a well used track and is designated on the map as a by-way open to all traffic. The walker is funnelled towards Glasbury Farm, where the nettles were head high when I walked this section in high summer. It is hoped that improvements in path maintenance can be achieved in this area.

Glasbury Farm, currently looking the worse for wear with the roofs of the farm buildings fallen in and the house needing some attention, is a sad sight. Surely someone will find it worth while to put it back in order, clearly it was once a well-built house and worth preserving.

From the farm the track improves enormously and a welcome return is made to the river. Follow the track, the mountains now more closely observed with the extreme steepness of their slopes better appreciated. After passing through a metal gateway leave the track as it swings away to the right and head across the grass towards the gateway seen ahead by a white house.

On reaching the road turn right to enter Glasbury village with telephone, post office, toilets (by bridge) and accommodation.

9: Glasbury to Hay-on-Wye

DISTANCE:	5 miles approx.
DETAIL:	Two modest hills with good views to the Black Mountains, long stretch of riverside.
MAPS:	1:25,000 Pathfinder 1038 (SO 03/13), SO 04/14 (Pathfinder 1015), Pathfinder 1016 (SO 24/34) 1:50,000 Landranger 161.
ACCOMMODATION:	Glasbury. Hay-on-Wye.
TOILETS:	Glasbury Bridge and Hay-on-Wye.
SHOPS:	Glasbury. Hay-on-Wye.
TOURIST INFORMATION:	Main car park, Hay-on-Wye. (0497 820144)

Glasbury (Y Clas-ar-Wy) is a quiet village with its riverside busy with the activities of eager canoeists, a river that in times past has destroyed its bridges, robbed the churchyard of its dead, and generally made life intermittently difficult for its inhabitants. The area has long been settled as the remains of past habitation noted on the map confirms. There is a Norman motte between the river and the road. On the higher ground south of the village a tumulus, (long barrow) a further motte and bailey and a simple "mound" are all faithfully recorded.

Each age leaves its mark on the landscape, some of them destined to be for ever enigmas to entertain and perhaps frustrate the archaeologists. Barrows which honoured the dead, the remains of field systems that fed the living, stone circles and man-made hills, hill forts and linear earthworks all chart the past. The "linear earthworks" of our day are derelict canals and abandoned railway lines, the veins and arteries of a transport system that has seen rapid change in the past 150 years. A line that served Glasbury, and is shown on the map south of the river, was the successor to a horse-drawn tramway constructed in 1816 to move heavy goods, coal in particular, from Brecon via Talgarth to Hay-on-Wye and into Herefordshire. Powys County Council has published a leaflet briefly describing the story of the tramway which can be obtained from tourist information offices. A graphic picture of the old line is depicted on the Tramway Inn at Eardisley, with two heavy horses hauling two trams loaded with coals against a background of the Black Mountains.

The origins of the village's name give a clue to its antiquity, Y Clas-ar-Wy, indicating a monastery. The foundation dating from the fifth century and dedicated to Saint Cynidr is believed to have been a little away from the present village at Ffynnon Gynydd. The eleventh-century church was too close to the river to survive, being regularly inundated by flood waters and eventually cut off by a change in the course of the river in the seventeenth century. Wiser counsels prevailed with the building of a new church on higher ground beyond the south bank of the river. A castle, somewhat later than appeared strictly necessary for the needs of defence, was built in the mid-nineteenth century at Maesllwch. Kilvert records that its owner kept a fearsome baboon which so alarmed visitors that they took flight.

The Walk

Take the path on the northern side of the bridge (dual signing in Welsh and English), cross a stile and head downstream with a fence between you and the river. A little beyond the sewage works, pass through a kissing gate and continue along the riverside through a short field with three ancient oaks. After a further kissing gate cross the bottom of another short field with a fence to your right. Again exit by a kissing gate and turn immediately right to pass through a metal gateway, then left to continue downstream, now with the fence to your left on a narrow path. When the next fence is crossed, join a broad but overgrown track.

After 100 yards leave by a kissing gate on your left, here swing diagonally left with the path heading to a large oak tree. In sixty paces a sign directs you left to cross the road by a five-barred gate. Once over the road go through a wooden kissing gate to follow the field boundary to exit onto the road, the A438, and turn right with it, the grassy verge allowing a retreat from the traffic.

In a little over a hundred yards a sign indicates the Maesyronnen Chapel, not on our route and reached in half a mile by way of a steep hill. A rather longer diversion than the mile return journey is required if the chapel is to be viewed properly, since the key has to be collected from a house

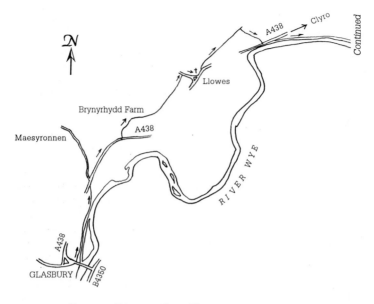

some way distant at Ffynnon Gynydd.

Maesyronnen Chapel

The long low building, with a sundial over the door, remains pretty much as it did in 1696 when it was extended from a small farmhouse to provide a nonconformist place of worship which is still in use today. If curiosity takes you off route to pay a visit, then it is as well to note now that the key has to be obtained from the Old Post Office at Ffynnon Gynydd a further mile up the lane. It is possible to peer through the windows, to glimpse its dark and comfortless wooden furniture, which like many a more recent church pew may have the effect of keeping you awake but is not calculated to keep minds on higher things for over long before the hardness factor begins to take effect. Perhaps this accounts in a measure for the enthusiasm for hymn singing since this activity is invariably carried out standing

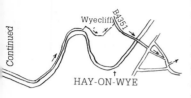

up. Be that as it may, it was not for the first time on the journey down the Wye that I wondered whether Psalm 121 which opens with the words "I will lift up mine eyes unto the hills" was not especially appropriate - for there is a fine view across to the Black Mountains.

The chapel is worth more than a peep through its windows, and some brief impressions may set the scene for the worship that has been carried on at this remote spot for 300 years. "Praise God in his Sanctuary" is written in large letters on the wall which adjoins the cottage; here the cruck construction of the long house is clear.

When I visited it the interior was sweet smelling; baskets of pot-pourri hung from the ceiling beams and a hop vine had been twined round the uprights. Twin candles stood either side of the five-inch thick bible, with herbs hanging down, rosemary and sage. Were they here for their scent or something more significant? Rosemary for remembrance and sage for wisdom, I thought. Remembrance was probably right but in the language of flowers sage is a symbol of domestic virtue, the House of the Lord swept and garnished.

Blackies Imperial Family Bible, dated MDCCCXLIV - 1844 - stood open at the last reading, its pages carrying out the promises of its publishers, "illustrations with a superb series of engravings from the most admired productions of ancient and modern art". Beneath the lectern the Ministerial Accession is headed "Commonwealth Era. Llanigon and Glasbury, Richard Powell 1647-1658". The names that follow could hardly be more Welsh - Owen Griffith, Evan Evans, John Griffiths, Lewis Rees, Rees Davies and so on - you can almost hear the echo of their sermons ringing round the building.

A bench carries the inscription AP 1728. The floors, like some of the memorials, are of slate. David Williams, who died November 12 1851, is remembered with the words:

Mark the perfect man, behold the upright,
for the end of that man is peace.

His daughter Anne, who died before reaching her majority, has a memorial that is a mix of sadness and hope -

> *My time was short on earth, My friends the more desired,*
> *But when God's pleasure was fulfilled, Then all my days expired.*

A life that was measured to the full was that of the Rev David Jones, who died in September 1849 at the age of eighty-three, after fifty years as pastor at Maesyronnen:

> *He began early, continued late, and met with storms*
> *and enemies of the most malignant kind,*
> *yet stood firm his ground and did cry Hallelujah.*

Communion in this little chapel is taken, not kneeling at an altar rail as is the custom in so many places of worship, but seated around a large oak table, the family gathered together with the minister at the head of the table, a full meaning of communion. The first impressions obtained through the window of "dark and comfortless" must be revised for here the people of this corner of Wales have surely found a place of peace and renewal.

The Walk Continued

From the junction to Maesyronnen, continue with the A438 where a fine stand of poplars, four deep like a column of soldiers on parade stands bolt upright, smartly to attention in their green livery. At a loop in the road an old milestone signals Hereford 24 miles, Glasbury 1. Many of the milestones that remain today, often hidden by the encroaching vergeside growth, date back to the days of the turnpikes. Not that these were an invention of the engineers who laid out the toll roads, for the Romans were accustomed to mark the distances by stone pillars.

After about half a mile of road walking a No Through Road is seen on the left; join it as it winds uphill quickly providing ever improving views over the valley of the Wye to the Black Mountains and a small snap shot back to Glasbury and its bridge. The lane becomes a track passing through the yard of Brynyrhydd Farm. The name of the common above is spelt the same but separated by hyphens - thus Bryn-yr-Hydd; struggling with a short glossary of Welsh names I deduced this to be Stag Hill; an exercise that, appealing though it is, I would be wiser not to attempt too often for even with a fuller dictionary there must be many a pitfall into which the unwary and ignorant Englishman will tumble headlong.

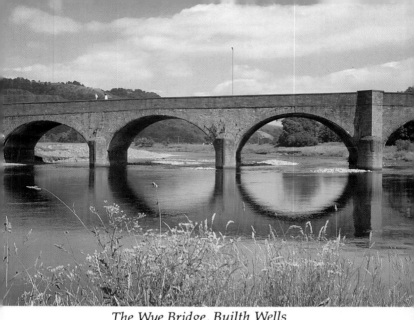

The Wye Bridge, Builth Wells
Llowes village

Hereford Cathedral from the river
Ross-on-Wye from the river

From the farmyard continue with a stone wall to your right which soon comes to an end. This is another good spot to pause and take in the view with the patterning of the farmed landscape rising gradually, before taking a dramatic leap up the steep slopes to the mountain tops. At the end of the wall note the waymark which indicates a direction that is slightly diagonally right, but clearly impossible at this point. The significance of this is soon revealed.

Walk on for fifty paces to swing half-right on a narrow indistinct path which drops downhill to a line of trees. Here turn left, again narrow and with the view blocked for a while. Maintain a north-easterly direction with the path improving and glimpses of the hills again permitted. By an ash tree continue on where there may be obvious signs of the path having been cleared with the improved path terracing the hillside. After passing through a clump of trees and a patch of bracken emerge into the open to look forward to the little village of Llowes and its church.

Cross a stile into a field and go forward, descending a bank, and slightly right, to the corner of the next field. Follow the path with fence on your left to a metal gateway to exit onto the road and turn right. Here a sign announces in English and Welsh that this is (or was, when judged) the "best kept small council house estate in Radnorshire".

Continue into the village to cross a bridge over a small stream, to reach the church of Saint Meilig, with its clock stopped either at the tea time hour of 4.20 or rather less appealingly at the crack of a summer dawn.

Francis Kilvert

It is here that we encounter a small sundial set close to the church path to commemorate the diarist, the Rev Francis Kilvert, and his association with the parish during the years 1865-79. Kilvert, long after his death, has become something of a literary figure, following the publication of what remained of an extensive set of diaries. He wrote with a poetic elegance which still reads well 120 years later.

Robert Francis Kilvert was Wiltshire born and following his father's vocation went into the church. He took up the curacy at Clyro in 1865, an office he held until 1872. Later he was vicar at Saint Harmons, north of Rhayader, and from 1877 to his death was vicar of Bredwardine, not so very far away in Herefordshire. Kilvert died at the early age of 39, a victim of peritonitis. Here was a man who greatly loved this border country that we are exploring and committed much detail of his travels and work to his notebooks. Like the village doctor, the parson knows everyone from the highest to the lowest; no-one is better placed to record the life and times of a small community. Like another famous clergyman diarist, the Rev Francis White of Selbourne, he enjoyed the beauties of the countryside and wrote daily of what he had seen and done.

Between 1938 and 1940 selected passages were printed in three volumes with an abridged version appearing later which is still readily available as a Penguin paperback. What a wealth of material there must have been in the missing volumes that would have been of value to social historians and have further delighted today's readers!

Kilvert crops up here, there and everywhere along our journey. Almost impossible to resist the irreverent temptation to parody the rather too well known graffitti with "Kilvert was here". He may be counted as one of us for we read of him taking long walks over the hills. He is found taking part in the social life of the area, taking tea at Hay Castle, playing croquet at Clifford Priory, dining with a fellow minister at Llowes. He had a care for the people of his parish, not just the well-off, but the old, the sick and the poor.

The dedication of the church to Saint Meilig comes strangely to ears more accustomed to a string of Saint Marys and Saint Johns, so this godly man requires a brief introduction. Meilig, abbot and confessor, was a Scot by birth but left his native land, founding a monastery near Llowes some time around AD 650. The church itself, whilst rebuilt in Victorian times, has its origins about that time and is amongst the oldest in this part of Wales. It houses a pre-Norman font cut from a solid block of stone by the monks of nearby Brynrhydd. For many years the font saw service as a garden ornament in one of the village houses but was returned to the church in 1955.

At the back of the church stands the great cross of Saint Meilig, fully seven feet high and weighing three and a half tons. For 500 years it stood upon the hillside, set up, we may suppose, by the monks to announce their arrival or as a monument to honour the founder of their monastery. Some time in the twelfth century, the cross was removed from its hill top site to the churchyard were it remained until 1956 when it was brought into the church. After

1,300 years of exposure to all weathers one cannot but congratulate the mason for the expert selection of the stone and his careful work that has left the cross of Saint Meilig in such remarkably fine condition.

The Walk Continued

Return to the village street and turn left to reach the main road. Here turn left and after passing the old school, pass through the metal gateway on the left, and in a few yards turn right through a further gateway to head uphill half diagonally right on a wide grassy track. (There is also an exit at the back of the churchyard via a kissing gate which will connect with our route.)

Again there are views of the Black Mountains and a rock by the path provides a suitable place to pause for refreshment and enjoy the view. The track rises to pass through a neck of woodland; at the end of the field beyond this, go forward to a stile and continue with a hedge on your left, again with good views. At the end of this field exit by a metal gateway and turn immediately right on a track which runs downhill with a tiny spring-fed stream to keep you company. Keep with the wide track, soon to meet and pass through a metal gateway, which curves to the right to meet the road. As you head downstream a rural picture beloved by artists of past generations may meet your eye, cattle drinking from the river.

When the road is met, the A438, turn left and cross to the lay-by seen a short distance ahead, at the end of which joining the path which runs parallel with the road for about 100 yards. Cross the stile on your right to join the riverside path which is followed downstream for over one and a half miles. With no concentration required on wayfinding, time can be given to enjoying the life of the river, keeping a sharp eye open to see what puts in an appearance.

The spot where the river is joined is popular with swans; a heron is almost certain to be seen, swallows and swifts swoop low over the water, a fish leaps to catch a fly, and if you are lucky perhaps you may enjoy one of those split-second electric blue flashes as a Kingfisher darts past. Buzzards may be seen hunting over the fields that border the conifer plantations on the hills to your left.

The river flows wide and shallow, but debris piled on the banks or caught in tree branches is a reminder of its volatile nature when the snow melts in the hills or heavy rains quickly bring it into spate. To the right the hills make a fine backdrop to the scene and the village of Clyro, for ever associated with Kilvert, is passed away to your left.

When the river starts to loop to the right to tumble over a weir, Hay church will be glimpsed. Near here, at a stile a stone commemorates a local fisherman and offers some piscatorial advice:

> *To the memory of Bill Barker 1894-1953*
> *who killed many salmon opposite this stone -*
> *Fish here in high water brother angler and you will do likewise.*

Cross the stile by the scene of Bill Barker's triumphs and continue along the bank with the tumult of the weir becoming louder. As it is approached the path pulls away from the river edging the grounds of a house to emerge onto a track which is followed for about 100 yards. Turn right over a plank bridge and stile to head half-right through a fir plantation. Cross a stile and continue uphill on a narrow path, rather dark under trees, soon with a high wall to your left.

As the wall falls back turn left over a stile to follow the other angle of the wall, with Hay, its church, bridge and castle coming into view. Follow the fence line as the wall comes to an end, and when it turns sharp left, do likewise following it to meet the road.

Turn right down the road to cross the bridge, pausing to enjoy the view downstream. At this point we are joined by the Offa's Dyke Path which, having made a long traverse over the Black Mountains by way of the Hatterall Ridge, has descended near Hay Buff to head for the little town. You will see it signed off downstream on the next stage of its 168-mile exploration of the border country between Sedbury Cliffs on the Severn and Prestatyn in North Wales.

At the road junction turn right into the centre of Hay-on-Wye to discover the perhaps unexpected delights of this little town.

10: Hay-on-Wye

Hay-on-Wye is a fascinating place by any standards, for in this little Welsh border town has been assembled the past, the present, and even something of the future of the world's history - all by virtue of its emergence as the country's second-hand book capital. This unique status for a small country town is part of its recent history but before we can browse through some of the millions of books that line miles of shelving the clock must be turned back a century or two.

Hay is mindful of the power of the river that flows past its doorstep and, fearful of getting its feet wet, quickly lifts its skirts and climbs the hillside to safety. Well it might, for the Wye in anger, as we have already learnt, is no respecter of man or his property. Its story is told with repeated references to the death of one and the destruction of the other. There are legends that assert the river must have its quota of sacrifices each year. Wide though it is, the shallow waters forbade navigation by cargo-carrying boats except when in spate. Barges or trows, hauled by men, were used to bring heavy goods to the town but clearly the state of the river dictated the opportunity and in such circumstances delivery on time could not be relied upon. One heavy item that seems to have made the long journey from Chepstow was the new bell ordered for the church in the eighteenth century. Hauling heavy goods upstream against a strong flow sounds like hard work indeed. Hard work on the river, but now for fun is the annual 100-mile raft race to Chepstow, a three-day event which takes place at Spring Bank Holiday. Notices in the town remind competitors that the local chemist's shop opens early to provide skin hardening lotions and similar medication.

The town sits on a hill looking out to the green hills to the north across which the Offa's Dyke Path makes a passage and to the south the Black Mountains over which it has already made a long traverse by way of the Hatterall ridge. Here the table-topped summits rise to over 2,000 feet and may be explored from the little, winding road that makes a long and not unexciting journey by Gospel Pass and the Vale of Ewyas to Abergavenny. Legend has it that Saint Peter

Hay-on-Wye - a town of books and the almost inevitable clock tower

and Saint Paul came this way to spread the gospel of Christ - an unlikely story, but one which has at least a strong spiritual connection. In this remote and sparsely populated area a religious community was established at Llanthony at the beginning of the twelfth century.

Hay is a tangle of narrow streets and alleys, built long before any consideration had to be given for the convenience, or otherwise, of the motor car. It can be a dark and brooding place, as if still mourning some of the black days of its past, when heavy tears are shed from the clouds that have raced over the mountains - a town that time has forgotten. Just as quickly its mood changes as the sun comes out, the tourists flock in and it is vibrant and alive once again, never more so than during the annual festival of literature when luminaries of the world of books mingle with the crowds and the sound of music echoes through the streets and alleyways.

The church of Saint Mary lies a little away from the main town and close to the green mound which was the site of the town's first castle, a Norman motte built around AD 1100. It is a neat little church, largely rebuilt in 1833 but with the squat tower remaining as a link to earlier times. Another and rather strange relic is tucked away under the stairs to the gallery - a much the worse for wear stone figure of a monk but sometimes referred to as the effigy of Maud Walbee, otherwise known as Maud De St Valerie. Its presence in the church seems almost an embarrassment, a figure without a proper place in the scheme of things, waiting for the moment when a decision might be made as to its proper accommodation.

Legend has it that the town's second castle, dating from AD 1200, was built by Maud in the course of a single day. In the midst of her herculean labour she momentarily paused to remove a stone which had lodged in her shoe. She angrily hurled the stone in the direction of Llowes where it landed in the churchyard. It must be assumed the lady took rather a large size in footwear for we are asked to believe that this was the stone that the Wye Valley walker will have already inspected at Llowes, to wit Saint Meilig's Cross.

Situated as it is the troubles of the border country could not have been expected to pass the town by. The castle that afforded protection to the town that grew up around its walls also served to make it a target and it became the subject of hostile attention on a number of occasions with successive rebuildings required.

It was attacked by King John in the year following Magna Carta during his continuing trouble with his barons and put to the torch by Llywelyn in 1231. Money was raised by local taxation to help protect the town by the building of an encircling wall but the troubles continued. In 1264 Prince Edward, Henry III's son stormed the castle only for the situation to be reversed in the following year by Simon de Montford. There was further conflict in the town in the next century when the castle was claimed for the crown and in 1402 it was again overrun, this time by Owen Glendower.

Even before these troubles the area was involved in the conflicts between the Normans and the Welsh. One such confrontation gave rise to the oft-quoted legend of the river of blood. Not in this case the Wye but the little Dulas Brook which marks the boundary between England and Wales. Bernard de Newmarch, who came over with the Conqueror, had established himself in Herefordshire and later in Brecon. An attempt to oust him by Rhys ap Tewdwr, King of South Wales, culminated in a decisive and bloody battle fought beneath the heights of Hay Bluff in 1093. Rhys and his sons were killed, and such was the carnage the story handed down to successive generations claimed that the little brook ran red with blood for three days.

The Rev Francis Kilvert, living over the river in the days of his curacy at Clyro, makes many references to the town in his diaries, of the May hiring fair, of cattle and sheep being driven along the lanes to the town and of social visits to Hay Castle.

Hay would have been a busy place on market day, not just the clamour of the cattle market with the farmers looking for the best price for their livestock but their wives busy at the butter and cheese markets.

But it is for books, particularly second-hand books, that Hay is famed today as it pursues a new and unlikely existence as a major home of the second-hand book trade, accommodated here, there and almost everywhere. A considerable local industry founded by Richard Booth, whose first bookshop was symbolically established in 1962 in the old fire station, for the business was to spread like wild fire. Books are big business in Hay and are to be found floor to ceiling in buildings that once had such diverse uses as a Victorian butcher's shop and a twentieth-century cinema. The last is a nice reversal of roles you may think, given the implied threat posed by the arrival of the celluloid age.

If you have ever wondered what happened to old books, you need never wonder again for clearly they do not die, many of them finding their way to Hay to be browsed through, sold and loved again - books of all descriptions and prices, from pence to those commanding high prices, humble paperbacks and great leather-bound tomes on every subject imaginable. Shops are devoted to specialist subjects like the performing arts, antiquarian books, music, theatre, cinema and dance. Others feature children's books, ecology, American poetry... There is a military bookshop, science fiction and horror books. Most are open every day of the year except Christmas, one goes even better with shelves open all night and an honesty box.

The silver screen, once thought the enemy of the written word, gives way to black print on white page at the former cinema. Here people browse through shelves set out in the garden, presided over by a pyramid of books. Fifty pence will buy almost any volume here, twelve for £5 - you could start a library with a modest sum. Inside seemingly endless miles of shelves are weighed down with the wordy outpourings of the literate world from the works of Shakespeare to the modern day detective novels of Georges Simenon. The *Life of Nelson* stands close to a volume devoted to the prehistory of East Africa. If the book you seek cannot be found, fear not, for specialists can be engaged to track it down for you.

Whatever you may make of the turmoil and unlikely stories of its past, you may remember Hay for its present, as the town where books from a million libraries come to be resurrected.

Note: A detailed leaflet on the second-hand and antiquarian book and print sellers of Hay is available at the tourist information centre in the town's main car park.

11: Hay-on-Wye to Bredwardine

DISTANCE:	9 miles approx.
DETAIL:	Pleasant walking on quiet lanes and field paths with fine views from Merbach Hill.
MAPS:	1:25,000 Pathfinder 1016 (SO 24/34) 1:50,000 Landranger Sheet 148.
TOILETS:	Hay-on-Wye
SHOPS:	Ditto.
ACCOMMODATION:	Hay-on-Wye. Bredwardine.
TOURIST INFORMATION:	Main car park, Hay-on-Wye. (0497 820144)

The many pleasures of the bookshops of Hay must be forsaken as the traveller ties his bootlaces and hefts his rucksack onto his shoulder once more.

From the town clock at the junction with Broad Street, head up Lion Street to meet the street signed Heol-y-Dwr. Here turn right and continue as far as the Old Black Lion, a coaching inn whose sign claims origins dating back to 1380. Turn left down a narrow street, no more than a path, and when this divides ignore the left fork and go forward to a small open space by houses.

Cross the Dulas Brook by the footbridge and in doing so leave Wales and Powys for England and Herefordshire. Take the path half-left up a bank and then head across a field to a tree-lined boundary. Here the path dips down to a stream with a waymark directing you to the right. Cross the stream and pass through a gateway to bear left up the bank by a large oak tree.

(A steeplechase of fields and stiles now follows, tedious in text but it must be included for completeness).

Cross the field to a gateway and stile seen opposite. Beyond the stile is a seat to commemorate the Queen's Silver Jubilee in 1977. From the seat head up the lane for a short distance. As it bends sharply to the right, take the path on the left which passes a bungalow on your left, and go forward to a stile.

Once over the stile follow the field edge with a hedge to your right. Exit by a stile and continue still with the boundary on your right. Almost at the end of this field cross a further stile by a large oak tree and make your way slightly diagonally right to an angle of hedge seen ahead. It was in this field that we saw a handsome fox - rich dark chestnut in colour - he passed close to a flock of sheep but they never stirred nor favoured him with a second glance. Nor he them!

From the hedge corner, follow the fence line to reach a further stile and again follow the field edge still with a wire fence to your left. At the end of the field cross a stile to turn right with a track - an avenue of fine oaks. In about eighty paces turn left to cross a field and meet a stile. Once over the stile go forward with a wire fence on your right, to cross a brook, choked by an intense growth of hairy willow-herb standing as tall as a man. Culpepper recommends willow-herbs in general for stemming the flow of blood and the marsh willow-herb was particularly mentioned in the treatment of one of the, what we sometimes less explicitly called, social diseases.

Carry on to cross a stile and narrow edge of field to the exceptionally high stile opposite and to cross the track leading up to Summer Hill Farm. Beyond the track bear diagonally right to meet a metal gateway and turn left for about thirty paces along the fence line, then right to follow the field edge to the gateway at the corner of the field. The Hardwicke Brook is to your left, hidden beneath a long belt of trees.

Pass through the gateway, which is found by a small clump of larch trees, and continue forward still with the fence line to your left. To your right will be seen a small, crenellated tower. Its isolated situation prompts speculation. What is it? - the remains of a church, a defensive tower or an expensive folly? None of these, for it is a nicely disguised water tower built around 1820 and now a Grade II listed building. The tree-covered hills beyond conceal earthworks and the remains of the motte and bailey of Mouse Castle, surely a stately home which ought to feature in *Wind in the Willows* or one of Beatrix Potter's stories.

Leave the field via a stile by the remains of an old stone wall with the path now heading a little to the right to meet a stile in the fence ahead which is found about half-way up the far field boundary. Once over stile head half-right to meet a boundary hedge and follow this (on your right). Towards the end of the field the track divides; ignore the way diagonally right and

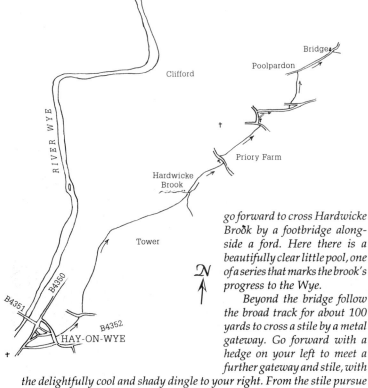

go forward to cross Hardwicke Brook by a footbridge alongside a ford. Here there is a beautifully clear little pool, one of a series that marks the brook's progress to the Wye.

Beyond the bridge follow the broad track for about 100 yards to cross a stile by a metal gateway. Go forward with a hedge on your left to meet a further gateway and stile, with the delightfully cool and shady dingle to your right. From the stile pursue the track to reach a further gateway and continue through a meadow to meet the lane by Priory Farm. A large and ancient oak stands by the gate, consumed by age and a wasting disease, its poor state of health not improved by the black charring which suggests that it has been the victim of lightning.

Turn left up the lane and in 100 yards turn right over a cattle grid to follow the footpath which passes to the north of Priory Farm with its large stone-tiled barns. The outlines of fish ponds recorded on the map remain as a reminder that this was once the site of a monastery.

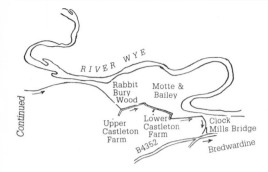

On the hill to your left will be seen the tower of Saint Mary's Church and below the ridge, out of sight and close to the Wye, are the remains of Clifford Castle. Here we encounter the echo of a royal liaison of 800 years ago that has all the elements of an historical

Hardwicke Brook

romantic drama that any writer of that genre could wish.

Clifford Castle was the birthplace of Henry II's most favoured mistress, the Fair Rosamund, daughter of Walter de Clifford. Many are the legends that have grown up around their association. Henry (1133-89) is probably best known to the general reader for his conflict with Thomas à Becket which led to the archbishop's murder on the altar steps of his cathedral at Canterbury. He married Eleanor of Aquitaine; two of their sons are especially remembered - John of Magna Carta fame and the crusading Richard the Lionheart. Despite having seven sons by the marriage, Henry was not adverse to seeking the pleasures of the bed elsewhere and he is reputed to have had several mistresses.

The Fair Rosamund, daughter of the Wye-side castle, was his clear favourite, a woman whom he might have married had he been free to do so. Their liaison was a long one.

Legend has it that Rosamund was hidden away from Eleanor in a secret chamber at Woodstock - the tabloids today would call it a love nest. Rosamund died at the early age of thirty-seven, much grieved over by Henry. How she died is not clear - later writers maintain that she was murdered by Eleanor, poisoned or being bled to death. Both stories, rumours might be a better word, have currency and are apparently equally unproven as are the claims that she had one, or perhaps two, sons by the king - Geoffrey, who was to become Archbishop of York and William Longsword, Earl of Salisbury.

Proof of Henry's great affection is found in her burial in the convent at Godstow on the Thames near Oxford, where she was accorded a place of honour in the chancel. The king and her father were both generous in gifts to the nunnery presumably in return for the sisters' devotions at her tomb. It seems strange to think of celibate nuns praying at the tomb of a king's mistress. Certainly it was not something that found favour with the saintly Bishop of Lincoln, Hugh, who owed his position to Henry. Hugh was a strong and upright man of the Church with a reputation for standing up to his royal patron. When visiting Godstow a year or two after the death of the king he found Rosamund's tomb candlelit and bedecked with rich fabric by the nuns in pursuance of Henry's wishes.

Offended that such a place of honour should have been afforded to a paramour the Bishop insisted upon the removal of her tomb to a less conspicuous location. Rosamund was to suffer one last indignity, indirectly at the hands of another Henry, for with the Reformation her tomb at Godstow was destroyed.

Continue with the rising path to the stile seen in the hedge at the top of the field. Beyond the stile go diagonally left to the top corner of the field to follow a narrow, hedged path to meet the cross roads in about 40 yards. Take the road signed to Clifford and Whitney on Wye; at the top of the rise the path is waymarked over (at the time of writing) rather derelict playing fields, but it is easier to carry on a few yards to the next road junction where you turn right.

The Calvinistic Methodist Chapel of 1827 is passed on your left, supported by an iron corset. Despite the peeling paint on its doors a neatly kept border in the churchyard confirms that this is still a regular place of worship. A Victorian pillar box, somewhat cobwebbed, is set in the stone wall by the chapel. What a good bargain these old pillar and letter boxes proved to be.

Follow this quiet lane along the high ridge for just over a quarter of a mile, passing Porking Barn with a pig on its sign and ignoring the first turn left. On reaching the house Cear Dene (seen on the right) take the track on the left which runs downhill towards a white cottage. Just before the cottage take the path signed to its right. The first few yards are overgrown and lead to a stile and on into a field. Bear half-diagonally right over the field to a stile at the corner. Beyond the stile follow the field edge, cross a brook and continue to meet the road by Pool Pardon Cottage.

Turn right to follow the road for 600 yards in all. About 200 yards after passing The Farm an old railway bridge is approached. Here bear right on a path currently signed "Permissive Route pending consideration of diversion order". Pass through a metal gateway to join the old railway track, now a pleasant green way set on a high embankment and running under trees.

As you emerge from the trees the Wye is seen below to your left. In 200 yards or so a further metal gateway is reached. Here leave the track to cross a stile on the left and follow the fence line on your right over the hillside. There is a fine view of the meandering Wye as it curves away from Whitney, with swans on the river and a good prospect of the opposite hills climbing above the valley. Whitney Bridge on the B4350 still requires payment of a toll to cross the river, a relic of the past which is now gaining modern currency as the government exacts a price for crossing the Severn or driving under the Thames.

Cross a stile at a field boundary and continue descending along the fence line with a gate and stile coming into view at the corner of narrowing field. Pass through the gateway to take the path through a belt of woodland with the Wye still below you on the left.

Leave the trees by a metal gateway and continue with a wire fence to your left, as the Wye starts yet another meander. Far ahead can be seen the high wooded slopes of Merbach Hill and Weston Hill Wood. Pausing here to take in the scene one August day we counted four cormorants flying upstream, a pair of herons, a dozen or more swans, some noisy mallards and a buzzard hunting over the fields beyond the east bank - a nice selection of the wildlife to be seen along the Wye, and all in a few brief seconds.

After an open stretch the path follows the outside edge of Rabbit Bury Wood for 150 yards then swings half-right, rising to meet a five-barred gate with Upper Castleton Farm seen to your right.

From the gate turn left down a quiet lane with verges wide enough to suggest that it might once have served as a drove road. After crossing a small stream the tree-covered mound of a motte and bailey is passed on your left. Lower Castleton Farm then Old Castleton is passed as the lane climbs.

At the top of the rise, as the lane curves to the left, take the footpath through the gateway found on your left. Follow the hedge line to a stile with the scatter of houses at Clock Mills coming into view, and Merbach Hill, knowing that it has yet to be climbed, looking distinctly steeper by the minute.

At end of the first field carry on along the headland to cross a stile and bear half-right to meet a drive, public bridleway, and go right with this to meet the road at Clock Mills Bridge. Here turn left and follow the road for a quarter of a mile. Ignore the first turn right which carries a sign for Burn House Barn - restaurant and accommodation - and a further sign for a Caravan and Camping Club listed site.

In a few paces take the track on the right signed Merbach. Thirsty travellers requiring refreshment may like to note that in a further 100 yards beyond the Merbach track is the Castlefield Inn. It has a colourful sign depicting a fair maid with a knight carrying a standard with a red cross. A nicely romantic picture - Rosamund and Henry II, - who else?

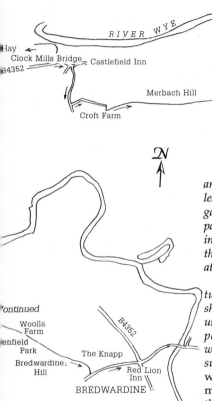

Follow the old green lane for 500 yards. Just short of Croft Farm a track comes in from the right; ignore this and go forward towards a No Through Road sign and turn left, again signed Merbach. In 200 yards the track turns sharp right to continue between green hedges, now rising steadily, with squirrels very active among the hazels and oaks. After a quarter of a mile leave the green lane by a five-barred gate and bear right to follow a rising path which reaches a boundary fence in 100 yards. Here and further up the hillside autumn crocuses flourish at the bracken edge.

Bear left up the hillside; at a turn a large stone surrounded by shattered snail shells indicates its use as a thrushes' anvil. The winding path climbs steeply through woodland and bracken towards the summit. As the trees fall back a wide view is presented, the Wye making a long looping course through the patchwork of fields, a chequer-board of beige, green or reddy brown according to the farming calendar, with the hills rising above the plain.

The bracken gives way briefly to a small patch of thistle, and the path becomes less distinct for a while. Maintain your direction to take a path which climbs alongside a gully. As you reach the small plateau below the summit ignore the path to the right and continue onwards and upwards on a narrow path. Merbach Hill is the steepest and longest sustained climb along the Wye Valley Walk and continues to terrace the hillside a little under its 1,043-foot summit. The view demonstrates how sparsely populated this area is.

Maintain your generally eastward direction, noting that there is a division of paths a little beyond the summit; the right, south-easterly route should be ignored. This heads towards Crafta Webb where Kilvert conducted his cottage lectures during his last incumbency at Bredwardine.

The wide path from the summit is pursued for 600 yards until the bracken gives way to farmland. At this point ignore the metal gateway seen ahead but turn right with the track for about forty paces. Then turn left on a narrow path through bracken and in a few steps cross a ditch and waymarked stile, to follow a path with the hedge to your right. Cross a further stile to go forward to a gateway and stile seen ahead. Here keep with the track which shortly follows the outside and southern edge of Westonhill Wood, to reach a corrugated iron farm building and pass through a metal gateway. This is sheep country.

Head half-right to pass through a former gateway by an ash tree. Here the land falls sharply away, again providing views to the east across the valley of the Wye. Follow the track towards Woolla Farm and as this is neared take the path beyond the stile on your right and follow it through the woods parallel with the lane to return to the track in 100 yards, having by-passed the farm.

Turn right to continue along the track with the wooded Benfield Park still on your right. After a quarter of a mile the path emerges into open fields, very probably occupied by brown and white Herefordshire cattle and black-eyed Friesians.

About 100 yards after leaving the wood forsake the wide track which leads to Benfield Farm and take the narrow path across the field - this is waymarked on a telegraph post. The path passes under The Knapp, 699 feet, briefly alluded to by Kilvert in his diary. When a gap in the hedge is reached, note the post and bear diagonally right to exit at the bottom right-hand corner of the field. Go forward over roughish ground with a hedge on your right. In just over 100 yards turn right through a metal gateway to join the track which meets the road in 100 yards.

Turn left to follow the road for 700 yards, descending a 1 in 4 gradient before reaching the Red Lion Inn on the B4352 at Bredwardine.

12: Bredwardine to Kenchester

DISTANCE:	7 miles approx.
DETAIL:	Points of special interest to be found at Bredwardine and Monnington with good river views for Brobury Scar.
MAPS:	1:25,000 Pathfinder 1016 (SO 24/34) 1017 (SO 44/54) 1:50,000 Landranger 149.
ACCOMMODATION:	Bredwardine. Byford. Hereford.
SHOPS:	Hereford.
TOILETS:	Hereford.
TOURIST INFORMATION CENTRE:	Town Hall Annexe, St Owens Street, Hereford. HR1 2PJ. (0432 268430)

Note: This section of the walk as described terminates at a possibly inconvenient point and walkers should consider continuing to Hereford as part of the day's travel. It also involves $2^1/_2$ miles of road walking between Byford and Kenchester as described in this chapter and a further $2^1/_2$ miles from there onwards until field paths and the river are rejoined - five miles which could be skipped if transport can be arranged. Purists devoted to walking every step of the way will quite rightly ignore this suggestion.

From the Red Lion at Bredwardine take the road forward, signed to Hereford. In 100 yards turn right on narrow lane signed to Bredwardine Church.

Bredwardine was the Rev Francis Kilvert's last ministry; he took charge of the parish in 1877 and perhaps this was where he was at his happiest. Here he had a parish, a house of his own, and seems to have quickly been taken to the hearts of his flock. His diaries tell of several local customs and legends; past sporting activities on The Knapp, reading between the lines some, at least, of a dubious nature; the Burning of the Bush to welcome New Year's Day and of

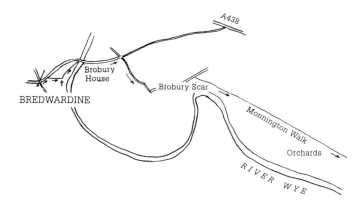

his visit to a hill top farm which greatly valued a tree reputedly a scion of the famous Glastonbury Thorn.

Bredwardine brought him the personal happiness of marriage, a marriage that was destined to be all too brief; in less than two months he died from peritonitis.

The second of the two quotations on his grave were to be strangely prophetic - five words from Saint Paul's epistle to the Hebrews - *He being dead yet speaketh.*

Readers who become engrossed in works of fact or fiction develop a picture of the writer or his characters. Kilvert's diaries are no exception and in reading his words we may feel that we have grasped the essential nature of the man and form our own mental image of him. Now is the moment of truth which will test how accurate that steadily building portrait is, for within the church is a photograph of the diarist. He is posing at a small table, dark of beard but fair of face, a bright and discerning eye you may think, a watch chain linked across his waistcoat and an open book in his hands - it would be tempting to think of this as his diary but there is nothing to encourage the viewer in this fancy.

The church is long and narrow, nowadays a place of peace receiving many visitors drawn here by the Kilvert connection. Several monuments provide interest beyond the Kilvert association. There is a tablet to George Jarvis -

*Munificent benefactor to the three parishes of Bredwardine,
Staunton-on-Wye and Letton - the poor of the parish grateful
for the liberal provision bequeathed to them in his will have caused
this monument to be errected out of the ample fund
appropriated to their use....*

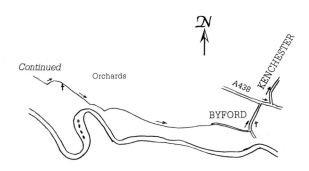

In essence of course he himself paid for this tribute to his generosity.

Memorials to those who die young have an inherent pathos; there are two such to be found here. The first, to the left of the altar reads:

*In memory of Harriet, daughter of Joseph and Elizabeth Thomas who
died 13th April 1778 in the sixteenth year of her age...
God taketh the good too good on earth to stay,
and leaves the bad, too bad to take away.*

The words reflect Defoe's assertion that the good die early and the bad die late. Also remembered is her sister:

*Mary who died 25th July 1785 aged 18...Here in simple virtue lies,
whose breath was snatched by early, not untimely death,
Hence did she go, just as she did begin, so to know before she knew to
sin. Death that does sin and sorrow thus prevent, is the next blessing
to a life well spent.*

In the chancel there are effigies of two giants of the past, one quite literally so, but much time-worn, the other one of Shakespeare's "happy few" who fought at Agincourt.

The Walk Continued

Return to the church gate and turn right to follow the narrow track which leads to the former vicarage. Here cross a stile with the Wye and Bredwardine Bridge coming into view. Head towards the bridge crossing a minor stream before reaching the road opposite the one-time toll keeper's cottage. Turn right and cross the bridge, pausing to enjoy the river and the distant view of Kilvert's white-painted vicarage.

Continue with the road soon passing Brobury House with its gallery and gardens open to the public. In 600 yards take the right turn (opposite Gypsy Lane). The lane is followed for about three-quarters of a mile, taking care when a T-junction is reached after 600 yards to keep left with the road.

When the edge of a patch of woodland is met in a further quarter of a mile, ignore the first turn right but take the next at the top end of the wood which is reached in 300 yards.

Soon there are fine views down to the Wye as it curves under the steep tree-clad incline of Brobury Scar. When the path divides take the left fork - the main track - but keep an eye open for the small track leading off left by an old gateway which is found as two ancient sweet chestnut trees come into view ahead.

The narrow track is followed only briefly to emerge into a field. Here turn right and follow the path along edge of two fields with woods to your right. At the foot of the second field pass through a metal gateway and turn immediately left to head south-east along Monnington Walk.

This is a handsome, motorway-wide avenue of trees, mainly Scots pine and yew with some oak. The avenue was planted in the seventeenth century, one account says to celebrate the restoration of Charles II to the throne in 1660. The excellent church guide suggests an earlier date and the marking of a different event, quoting the evidence of the tree rings. Perhaps both are true with trees being added to replace casualties or to extend the avenue. To the right of the avenue lies a huge expanse of apple orchards; there could be no better time to walk this way than in spring with the blossom blowing pink and white in the soft breezes of May. Readers of Kilvert's diaries may again experience a sense of *déjà vu* as they explore Monnington and note how well he described the avenue, Brobury Scar and the church now seen ahead.

Brobury Scar and the Wye

Half a mile after joining the avenue a gateway leads onto a metalled track - continue with this. At the top of the lane bear left as it swings past a house and over a cattle grid. Now turn right on a wide grassy path signed to Saint Mary's Church. Pass through a small metal gateway with Court Farm to your right. Here gaudy peacocks parade upon the walls, full of self admiration and anxiety to impress the dowdy hens in the garden below.

On then to the ancient lych gate and an even older yew tree to reach the church standing close to Court Farm and its large pond. There are many churches along the way, some locked, some not; time may forbid visiting them all but this is one not to be missed.

There is a timeless atmosphere within its light and airy walls, but spirit lamps serve to light the church for evensong as the nights draw in. The visitor is immediately struck by the handsome and quite exceptional three dimensional coat of arms of Charles II. How often in these quiet country churches stories are told of distant places when travel was far more an adventure than it is today! A prime example is the bust of Francis Perrott; his nicely rhymed memorial tablet tells how "...His native limits scorned to be confined" and recounts his valour on the high seas defending Venice against the raiding Turks in the seventeenth century.

Monnington has long been legendarily associated with the last resting place of Owen Glendower. After many years of conflict and often successful rebellion, his peaceful death around 1416 seems to have occurred without any firm indication of his burial place. The Monnington-on-Wye story is associated with the discovery of an old tomb in the churchyard which acquired the reputation of being that of Glendower. Again Kilvert readers will have the benefit of his words as in his typical fashion he briefly ponders upon the peace the old warrior had found beneath the churchyard trees.

Another hero of many a battle in the Napoleonic Wars is buried in the churchyard, William Williams, whose honours included Salamanca and Waterloo. Alas the headstone which told his story is cracked and crumbling and the visitor must rely upon the church guide for a full account of the inscription which recorded his long years of military service.

After visiting the church return to the lych gate and take the path that runs through the churchyard to exit past the pool at the bottom end. Here we are in the cider orchards of the famous Bulmer company of Hereford. A large notice "...welcomes Wye Valley Walkers to Monnington Orchards, 310 acres of cider apple trees representing part of the 2,000 acres grown by Bulmers throughout Herefordshire..." The board goes on to list the variety of apples grown in the orchard. Several types of apple are used in the production of cider; one small farmhouse cider bottler told me that he used at least ten varieties in his blends. The old tradition of providing a barrel of cider for workers in the harvest fields continues in the county. Bulmers products, under a variety of brand names, Woodpecker, Pomagne and Strongbow, make them the UK market leader.

The firm has been a growing part of the life of the city of Hereford since it was founded in 1887 by H.P.Bulmer, son of the rector of nearby Credenhill. The story of cider manufacture from its earliest farmhouse days to modern factory production is told in the Museum of Cider in Hereford.

Take the path with the hedge on your right and the orderly lines of apple trees on your left. Soon the Wye swings in to greet you again, another spot where you may see a heron fishing in the shallows. Continue along the boundary fence with the river to your right. In about 200 yards a notice "Permissive route pending consideration of a diversion order" directs you sharp left through a wide gap between the apple trees. In a further 200 yards the orchards are left behind and a footbridge crossed to emerge into a field with a hedge on your left. Follow the path which widens into a good track, still with permissive notices in evidence. The clear track is now pursued for a mile to meet a lane at Byford. Here turn left passing Byford Court on your left and the church on your right.

There are wall paintings to be seen in the south transept and memorials to various members of the Cotterell family. Tablets and benefactions of interest include the story of James Reade whose loyalty to Charles I led to his dismissal from his post as chaplain at New College, Oxford, following the battle of Edgehill.

In 1702 a Mr Aubrey Smith "...bequeathed twenty shillings per year to the poor of this parish from a piece of land called The Hales, to be divided amongst poor housekeepers not having weekly pay, payable on the Sunday next before Christmas Day for ever ...a piece of land adjoining the River Wye in the meadow called The Limpyaid, to find the bread and wine for the sacraments of this parish for ever."

In 1746 "Tamberlane Hords, late of the City of Hereford, gentleman,...devised to the minister and churchwardens of this parish and their successors forever a piece of ground near Bridgeweir in this parish in trust to dispose of the yearly rent or profits thereof to four poor housekeepers of this parish not receiving alms from the parish on Good Friday yearly by equal proportions being intended for buying them corn."

What pictures are painted here with these brief words; of the learned men of Oxford being sacked for their allegiance to the king during the bitter days of the Civil War, of poor housekeepers "not having weekly pay" being remembered by rich men in their wills with a benefaction to last for ever and of the funding of the Holy Communion long after the donor's bones had turned to dust.

From the church continue up the lane to meet the A438 and turn right to follow it for 150 yards. Now take the road on the left to pass through gateway by the lodge house. (A telephone is on the A438 near here - the opportunity to summon up a taxi if you intend to skip the long stretch of road walking and press on to Hereford which is seven

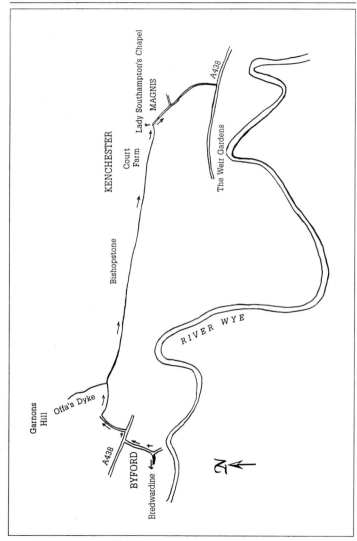

miles to the east.)

The lane runs through parkland with some ancient oaks and sturdy sycamores with the wooded slopes of Garnons Hill seen ahead. After a quarter of a mile the road swings to the right, following in the steps of the Roman legions. It takes a straight (ish) easterly course for two and a half miles parallel with the busy A438. Home Farm is passed beyond which a section of Offa's Dyke runs northward through the woods (the dyke it should be noted, rather than the long distance path which is not always faithful to the Mercian king's eighth-century boundary marker).

The trek along the Roman road passing Downshill House and the long straggle of Bishopstone comes to an end at the junction of roads with Kenchester downhill to the left and Lady Southampton's Chapel facing you as you arrive at the edge of the Roman town of Magnis.

13: Kenchester to Hereford

DISTANCE:	7 miles approx.
DETAIL:	Long stretches of road walking, mostly on pleasant lanes. Field paths and riverside complete the way to Hereford.
MAPS:	1:25,000 - SO 44/54 (Pathfinder 1017) & Pathfinder 1040 (SO 43/53) 1:50,000 Landranger 149
TOILETS:	Hereford
ACCOMMODATION:	Hereford
SHOPS:	Hereford
TOURIST INFORMATION:	St Owens Street Hereford HR1 2PJ (0432 268430)

The choice of Kenchester as an end to a walking section may seem odd, but is governed by the long stretches of road walking, mentioned in the last chapter, required before the river bank can be rejoined. It seemed appropriate to offer the possibilities of doing a "skip" and picking up a bus from Bishopstone, Kenchester or Credenhill; timetables must be consulted before selecting this option! The riverside approach to Hereford is enjoyable and you may think it is right and proper that the pilgrim arrives at the cathedral city on foot.

Kenchester is a tiny village, a little straggle of houses, one a former school, which runs down the hill to the left and not on our route. The towerless village church is found close to Court Farm. A nail-studded door gives access to the narrow candlelit nave, with an oddly shaped font that looks as if it has been converted to its present use from something else; which, indeed, it has, for it is Roman in origin. The church was restored in 1925 by Robert Parr, of the banking family, whose gardens at The Weir, off the main road, can be visited if time can be spared for a short diversion. You may find the fields around Court Farm serving as a nursery with many horses and foals, coming up to the fence to be admired.

The Route

Kenchester is approached by the lane from Bishopstone to meet a T-junction by Lady Southampton's Chapel. Here turn right down the lane signed to Hereford and Credenhill. In a short distance a house called The Walls is passed, with millstones set into its wall, but I wondered if the name was derived from its position on the edge of the Roman town of Magnis. A little way down the lane it is possible to scramble up the bank but there is nothing to be seen of the town that flourished here for 200 years from the middle of the second century. It was clearly of some importance, covering a site of some 22 acres, certainly bigger than today's Kenchester, and excavations have revealed walls up to six feet thick. One man's ancient monument, is another man's convenient and free supply of building materials, and it has suffered the same fate as Hadrian's Wall, for example, with stone being carried away to construct farms and houses in the area.

The map shows the Roman road running east to west across its entire length, passing the northern edge of Hereford. This road, or more correctly the line of the road, is still in partial use. It ran from Viroconium (Wroxeter) to Caerleon in Gwent where the legions had a substantial garrison from around the third quarter of the first century.

The Romans were not the first to live here, for beyond the fields the thickly wooded slopes of Credenhill conceal a substantial camp, over three times the size of Magnis. The modern village of Credenhill lies below and to complete the "military occupation" of the area, the RAF has a base here.

It is three-quarters of a mile from Lady Southampton's brick-built chapel to the main road, the A438, but an alternative route cutting off a corner is under consideration and may be signed off on the left part way down the lane.

The Weir Gardens, in the care of the National Trust, lie off our route, half a mile to the west along the A438 and are especially rewarding in springtime when the steep banks above the riverside are richly carpeted with a mass of flowering bulbs. Daffodils, although golden according to Wordsworth are found here in all shades through to pure white. Scilla, violets, and muscari bring in the blues that are such a strong feature of the early flowers, contrasting with the fresh green of the emerging willow and the white cottony

KENCHESTER

A438

Sugwas Pool →

N

Upper Breinton

† Lower Breinton

R I V E R   W Y E

A438

HEREFORD

Cathedral Wye Bridge

Hunderton Bridge

Victoria Bridge

Continued

flowers of the cherry, while primroses add a homely touch. A series of terraced and stepped paths provide fine views down to clipped yews and rock gardens bright with Japanese maple.

From the junction with the main road turn left to follow the A438 for just under a mile, passing a scatter of houses that includes the home of a model railway enthusiast who has a large track laid out in his front garden and the Kite's Nest Inn. The grass verge will provide some refuge from the traffic on this busy road. An escape will eventually be effected when a narrow lane signed Sugwas quarter of a mile and Breinton one and a half miles is signed on the right.

The roar of the traffic is quickly exchanged for a more pastoral scene, uneventful but pleasant walking along quiet lanes and old tracks to rejoin the river bank. The winding lane is followed for a mile and a quarter. At a bend it rises and there is a glimpse of the Wye below but you will be denied its company for some time yet. Wadworth Cottage, with the legend In memory of Alice Wadworth Jan 1, 1901 carved over the front window is passed and soon a small modern housing development is met with exceptionally well-kept gardens. Here you turn left on a narrow lane which soon gives way to a steadily rising rough track.

After passing a house at the top of the rise the track narrows to a path and in under 100 yards passes through a gateway into a field. Bear right along the field boundary on a wide track, gaining a little height with views opening up to the wooded hills to the north. At the end of the field pass through a metal gateway, leaving the boundary fence to maintain your eastward direction across a field with views to distant smoky blue hills, including a glimpse of the Malvern Hills, 20 miles to the east. A further metal gateway is reached to join a track running between hedges, again decorated with wild flowers, but the identification is left for the reader.

The lane at Upper Breinton is reached in 600 yards; here you turn right passing a pair of "black and white" cottages. On reaching a T-junction turn right and in 200 yards, just as the lane bends to the right, take the path on the left through a kissing gate, climbing a short steep bank to emerge into a field. Turn right to follow the field boundary to exit at the bottom end by a small stile. Continue with the hedge to your right. At the end of this second field pass through a kissing gate and turn right to meet the lane by Breinton Court Lodge.

Cross the lane and take the path opposite beyond a metal gate to head diagonally left across an orchard which is left by a further kissing gate into a lane. Here turn right passing the entrance to Breinton House with its handsome pair of ironwork stags' heads. In 100 yards pass through the National Trust's Breinton Springs car park by way of a wooden kissing gate that was not constructed to allow the passage of even a relatively slim man with a pack on his back. Away to the left, just visible through an orchard, is Saint Michael's Church. In a short distance the path swings to

Decorative deer at Breinton

the left and drops downhill to allow the walker a joyful reunion with the river which is followed for the next two miles to Hereford.

A wry smile of memory may be involuntarily prompted by the rope suspended from a tall tree which the local lads use to swing out over the river in commando style. The situation has been nicely summed up by someone for placed strategically at either side of this small, self-made adventure, are two lifebelt stations.

The fields along the river are mostly given over to grazing, high quality Freisian cattle, fresh and clean, ear-tagged and numbered on their rumps - a small indignity they do not recognise. Cattle have been fattened along these meadows for centuries, changes are inevitable and today's herdsman rounds up his charges with the aid of a mountain bike.

Along the river bank there are small clumps of Himalayan Balsam - Policeman's Helmet, as it is sometimes called - but not in the profusion that so often occurs where they take over almost to the exclusion of everything else.

The occasional Canada goose may be seen, by no means the great numbers that have so successfully colonised the Thames Valley. These birds, gregarious as a rule, are great survivors and it is strange to see just single birds here and there. Swans, majestic and graceful as ever, are more numerous; is it too late to change the collective noun to a "grace of swans"? This would be an unnecessary complication since they already have at least seven - drift, herd, bank, team, wedge, that's five - leaving two for the walker to puzzle over in the last mile or two close to Hereford.

That "civilisation" is close at hand is not in doubt; a golf course is located on the opposite bank and a sudden plop may signal a leaping fish or a not too well-judged stroke. Fly fishermen, too, exercise their skills, waist-deep in the swirling waters, casting their lines with great skill and artistry. Above the golf course, partly hidden by a clump of trees stands Belmont House, in part resembling a French château.

A succession of fields is pursued downstream and by the time the pump house is reached the central tower of Hereford Cathedral comes into view - and another tower. Hereford has many museums and the first of these is signalled by the red and cream bricks of the tower of the Herefordshire Waterworks Museum. The museum, proud of its Broomy Hill Engines, is housed in the Victorian Pumping Station, a little off our route but which can be visited directly from Hereford. Opening hours are limited but opportunities exist to see the great engines and boiler working by steam.

When a second pumping station is reached a notice by a sports field announces "Private Land", but continue as the path follows the edge of the ground to join a tarmac path. Soon a handsome bridge is met and crossed; today it conveys only those on foot or cycles but surely so fine a piece of engineering must have been dedicated to a more worthy use than mere plodders and peddlers? And so it proves to be, for this is the Hunderton Bridge, the design commissioned from Charles Lidell by the Newport, Abergavenny and Hereford Railway Company, and opened on January 2, 1854. It was rebuilt in 1913 by the Great Western Railway using Lidell's stone piers that formed the

*Hunderton Bridge once carried the railway. Now it is strictly
for cyclists and walkers*

foundation for the crossing. The line was eventually closed in 1966,
but an inspired city council purchased the bridge in 1981, renovated
and repainted it - and very handsome it looks, too. It would have
been a tragedy if, like some of the Wye railway bridges, it had been
sold for scrap.

*Once over the river continue downstream, pass under the modern road
bridge and onto the Wye Bridge, itself an ancient monument - in the very
best sense.* The bridge has been here since 1490 - 500 years of service,
an unequalled record for Wye bridges so prone to succumb to the
occasional fits of violence that seize the river but, not totally
uninterrupted service for during the Civil War one span was blown
up for strategic reasons. In common with many bridges, a gatehouse
stood at the approach to the city until 1782.

As at neighbouring Severnside Worcester, there is a fine view of
the cathedral from the bridge, a pressing invitation, if one is needed,
to explore this ancient and historic city.

14: Hereford

Hereford, as its name continues to proclaim, had its origin with the Saxon foundation of a small town at an ancient crossing of the Wye. Like the story of the favourite old axe which has had five new handles and three new heads each century has seen both additions and subtractions.

The first defences of earth banks were replaced by more lasting stone. A Norman castle, described by one sixteenth-century writer - perhaps for the benefit of his sovereign - as being nearly as large as Windsor, was built to assist in the protection of the notoriously uneasy borders with Wales. Had it survived, what a superb view from the river it might have provided for the Wye Valley Walker, castle and cathedral set side by side! Surely if ghosts walk in Hereford they do so on Castle Green which was also the site of the monastery named after an early eighth-century Mercian hermit - Saint Guthlac.

The foundation of the see in 676 is claimed to be amongst the earliest in the country. Hereford's first church gave way to larger buildings which were in turn rebuilt, restored and renewed, part of the succession of new handles and axe heads. The Wye bridge celebrated its 500th anniversary in 1990, a successor to the first stone bridge of AD 1100 which in turn had replaced one constructed in timber.

"The Welsh are coming, the Welsh are coming!" was a cry that was heard in the streets of Hereford in more than one century. Disaster struck a few years before the Norman Conquest when the Welsh, in yet another of their border forays, rampaged through the city looting and burning. The troubles were a continuation of the problems that had led to the construction of Offa's Dyke in 782, a boundary marker from the Sedbury Cliffs on the Severn estuary in the south to the River Dee in the north. There was further upset during the twelfth-century power struggle between Stephen and Matilda, when the house of God was used to assault the castle of man, a piece of military strategy which did not deserve to succeed although the bombardment from the cathedral tower secured the submission of Stephen's supporters in the castle. In the north of the county at Mortimer's Cross a decisive battle in the Wars of the Roses was fought in 1461 which led to the crowning of the Yorkist Edward IV and the execution in Hereford of Owen Tudor.

The tides of the Civil War which flowed back and forth across the Midlands did not pass Hereford by, with the city under siege for several weeks in the summer of 1645. It survived this onslaught only to succumb in December without any great resistance, taken by surprise or perhaps just too war-weary. Earlier, in April 1643, the town had been forced to surrender to forces under the command of William Waller, whose successful generalship had earned him the sobriquet William the Conqueror. Waller moved on to attack Worcester and the king's supporters were able to take charge of the town once more.

It is the cathedral that provides the continuing link down the years. The joint dedication to Saint Mary and Saint Ethelbert introduces a legend that finds tangible expression in the well near Castle Green. Ethelbert, an East Anglian king was betrothed to Elfrida, daughter of Offa, the powerful king of Mercia. In 794 the young king travelled to Herefordshire for the wedding but before it could take place Offa, fearing that his future son-in-law might prove to be a powerful rival, gave orders for the bridegroom to be beheaded. The murder had some unexpected consequences for it proved impossible to bury the body with discretion. Strange lights danced over the grave and a ghostly figure appeared instructing that Ethelbert should be re-interred at Hereford. The remains were transferred as commanded - such a request could scarcely have been ignored in those still superstitious days - where his tomb attracted the usual pilgrimages and stories of miraculous cures. The well stands on the spot where the king's severed head is said to have fallen whilst being moved to its last resting place and, as may be expected, acquired the usual reputation for healing properties.

The shrine of a later saint, Thomas Cantilupe, Bishop of Hereford between 1275 and 1282, may still be visited within the cathedral. He was a godly man to whom miracles were attributed after his death, leading to his canonisation in 1320. A magnificent new shrine was built in 1349 to rehouse the saint's relics which were moved to their new place of honour in the presence of a large congregation headed by Edward III. For 200 years Thomas's tomb was an object of veneration and pilgrimage until the Reformation of 1538 led to the wholesale destruction of such monuments...but Thomas was not forgotten. In 1982 the 700th anniversary of his death was celebrated by the erection of a nimbus above his shrine.

The cathedral has many treasures, one of which attracted world attention when in 1989-90 proposals were made for the sale of its unique map of the world in an effort to raise funds to effect essential and expensive repairs. The Mappa Mundi depicted the world as known in 1290, 200 years before Columbus discovered America. It was the work of Richard of Haldingham and Lafford, a prebendary of Lincoln Cathedral. He later moved to Hereford and bequeathed the map to the cathedral in 1313, a legacy which, thankfully, it still retains. Jerusalem is depicted as the centre of the world with the yet un-United Kingdom occupying a small corner of the map. The main cathedral cities appear upon the map as does the River Severn, Snowdon and Clee Hill...hardly the greatest of English heights.

An equal if not greater treasure is the chained library, the largest in the world. It is by any standard a fascinating place with over 1,400 volumes chained to bookcases made in 1611 and based on those in Oxford's Bodleian Library which dates back to 1480.

Hereford's collection is especially valuable; priceless would not be too strong an adjective, since like the shrines of the saints many libraries held in cathedrals and monasteries were lost or destroyed in the religious upheavals of the sixteenth century. The oldest book, the Saxon Gospels, predates the present cathedral by a considerable margin, and continues to be used during the services when bishops and deans swear their oath on their enthronement or installation... surely both an uplifting and humbling experience for those coming to great office in the service of the church. The book was left to the cathedral by Bishop Athelstan, a man who had devoted a great part of his life to building one of the predecessors of today's cathedral; a work of love and care that was to be destroyed within a short time of its completion when the rampaging Welsh wrought havoc in the town in 1055.

The county's long history of cider making, which is known to have existed before the Roman invasion, is nicely commemorated in

John Wycliffe's translation of the Bible completed in about 1380. Here the words "strong drink" are passed over in favour of "cider", thus bestowing upon it the somewhat irreverent title of "The Cider Bible". The illuminated sections, rich in blues, reds and golds, are almost as bright as the day they were penned. *The Golden Legend*, a volume of lives of the saints printed by William Caxton at his Westminster press in 1483 is virtually complete, only the pages relating to the martyred Thomas à Becket being missing. Another volume which contains the church services of the fifteenth century, *Officioe Ecclesioe,* includes a charm or prayer for the relief of toothache!

The library houses some other curiosities, including a triple-locking book chest and a wooden leg. This last requires some explanation. It belonged to Sir Richard Pembridge, Knight of the Garter, whose tomb is to be seen on the south side of the nave. Sir Richard was a veteran of the Battle of Poitiers in 1356 - not that he lost his leg in that great victory of the Hundred Years' War but some 300 years later. A replacement wooden leg was carved complete with the coveted garter honour, a classic mistake because members of that distinguished order wear only a single garter. The carver had fallen into the understandable trap of producing a right leg to match the left. The error was eventually corrected in the last century with the discarded wooden leg remaining as a curiosity and a lasting embarrassment to the perpetrator of the error. Sir Richard Pembridge served for many years as a soldier and was rewarded not only by his election to the Order of the Garter but by the lifetime grant of the custody of Southampton Castle and the New Forest. He was also the Constable of Dover, Warden of the Cinque Ports and a Royal Chamberlain.

The library cannot be left without mentioning that it was here that Admiral Nelson received the freedom of the city in 1803. The tall column erected on nearby Castle Green some six years later stands as a more lasting tribute to the man who is still regarded with much affection as our greatest naval hero.

The cathedral has a number of memorials to past bishops whose fortunes were closely linked to that of the city, like George Cope who was removed from his office for the crime of supporting the wrong side during the Civil War. Bishop Charlton also lived in troubled times, when the dread hand of the Black Death was more feared than the sword; it was he that had a cross erected in the city to give thanksgiving for the end of the scourge.

The Stanbury chantry chapel commemorates another Bishop of Hereford (1453-74). His problems arose from conflicting claims to the throne. John Stanbury was a distinguished man of letters at Oxford and confessor of Henry VI. He encouraged the king to found Eton College and was named as its first provost, an office he did not take up. His allegiance to Henry during the Wars of the Roses led to imprisonment in Warwick Castle following his capture at the Battle of Northampton in 1460. The stained glass windows in the little chapel depict events in his life including Eton College.

It is always good to find modern workmanship mixing with that of the past, such as the tapestries in the south transept, designed by John Piper to mark 1,300 years of worship in the cathedral. The musical heritage of the city is exemplified in the Three Choirs Festival, which alternates with the sister cathedrals of Gloucester and Worcester. For 300 years, singers, musicians and composers, not a few of world wide fame, have gathered in the three cities in a great and glorious celebration of music. Long may their voices echo round the ancient stones.

Amongst the city's several museums is The Old House. The three-storey jettied half-timbered house dates from about 1620 and is reputed to have been built by John Abel. Abel by name and able by nature, he had a considerable reputation as an architect of timber-framed buildings. His skills were used to good effect during the 1645 siege when he constructed an apparatus to grind corn. Charles I was sufficiently impressed to grant him the title of King's Carpenter.

Like his buildings, Abel lived to a ripe old age and was never idle. In his nineties he carved his own effigy and composed the words for his memorial tablet in anticipation of his demise. The last lines read:

> *His line and rule so death concludes are locked up in store,*
> *Build they who list or they who wist, for he can build no more,*
> *His house of clay could hold no longer,*
> *May heavens frame him a stronger.*

The Old House, a lasting tribute to his skills, was once part of Butchers' Row but now stands alone displaying many items of domestic furniture and equipment. There is a kitchen with a fire back of 1634 bearing the royal coat of arms and a spit designed to be turned treadmill fashion by a small dog. Its special interest is the assembly of wooden furniture. Beautifully polished tables, fine chairs, spinning wheels, four poster beds and oak chests all contribute to an enviable display of craftmanship. Curiosities include a door with a dog flap (nothing new under the sun), and a seventeenth-century "baby walker". A wooden panel in one of the bedroom settings depicts "The Law Suit" with two men in obvious dispute over the ownership of a cow. The unfortunate creature is the object of a tug of war with one claimant gripping its horns whilst the other grasps the tail. A gowned and bewigged attorney sits before the contestants in the certain knowledge that, whatever the rights and wrongs of the claims, he at least is sure to profit from the dispute.

A scale model of the city as it was prior to the Civil War shows both the castle and cathedral, the last still sporting the spire that was to prove too great a burden forcing its removal towards the end of the eighteenth century.

The city cannot be left without reference to some of its other famous sons and daughters, a list which seems to be dominated by the theatrical profession. Ladies first: Eleanor Gwynne, better known as Nell, was born in Pipewell Lane not far from the Wye bridge. She went to London in search of a career which began as an orange seller at the Theatre Royal, and progressed to the stage where she first appeared at the age of fifteen in a play by John Dryden. She is reputed to have had several lovers and attracted the attention of King Charles II by whom she had two sons. The first, born when she was twenty years old, was Charles Beauclerk who was later to be ennobled by the king, first as Baron Heddington and Earl of Burford and later as Duke of Saint Albans. A second son, James, was born on Christmas Day 1671, but did not survive to adulthood. The Chelsea, Royal Hospital, founded for army veterans by Charles, is sometimes said to owe its existence to the influence of Nell, a claim that is backed by the likeness of the uniform of the famous Chelsea Pensioners to the outfits of the almsmen of the Coningsby Hospital in the city. It seems churlish to cast doubts upon such a good story but elsewhere you may read that the hospital derived from a similar institution established in France a few years earlier with the famous uniform being based on those of Marlborough's armies.

The king is reputed to have lavished considerable sums upon his mistress during his life and among 'famous last words' he is oft quoted as saying "Let not poor Nelly starve".

By an odd coincidence two of the most famous actor managers were born in Hereford within four years of each other. David Garrick, son of an army recruiting officer, was born at the Angel Inn, in 1717. Having received his education at Lichfield Grammar School he travelled to London to seek his fortune with another great name of the day, the lexicographer Samuel Johnson. Garrick went into the wine business initially but it is not the quality of his cellar for which he is remembered but for his many Shakespearean roles and actor-managership at London's Drury Lane.

Following hard in Garrick's footsteps was Roger Kemble. His fruitful marriage to Sarah Ward, another member of the profession, produced twelve children of whom a number were associated with the theatre, notably Sarah Siddons. Kemble clearly believed in "keeping it in the family" and his travelling company included a number of his children in the cast.

A Hereford man who achieved what some might regard as eccentric fame was Alfred Watkins, the controversial author of *The Old Straight Track*. Watkins made a detailed study of the country's network of ancient trackways, and went into print to demonstrate his conclusions that many ancient sites, earthworks, beacon hills and the like lay upon the straight lines of the old tracks in an alignment with the sun. Ley line hunting became something of a fashion and readers of his book may find it adds an extra spice to their walking. Nor should he be dismissed as a crank, for he was a keen photographer with a practical and inventive mind and honoured by the Royal Photographic Society.

Today Hereford is a bustling, thriving market town, still an important crossing of the Wye. The age-old tradition of cider making continues as one of its biggest industries. The battles that are fought within its boundaries are now played out on the football field where the local side has sometimes found a role as giant killers.

15: Hereford to Mordiford

DISTANCE: 5¹/₂ miles approx.

DETAIL: Level walking with fine view of the
                          cathedral from the riverside. Lanes and
                          field paths.

MAPS: 1:25,000 Pathfinder 1040.
                          1:50,000 Landranger Sheet 149

TOILETS: Hereford.

ACCOMMODATION: Hereford. Mordiford. Fownhope.

SHOPS: Hereford.

TOURIST INFORMATION: St Owens Street, Hereford. HR1 2PJ
                          (0432 268430)

*Having sampled at least some of the delights and diversions of Hereford it
seems appropriate to set off on the next stage of our journey from the
cathedral, a starting point that may add something of a pilgrim image to
our travels. From the west front set off down King Street and then take the
first left, Bridge Street, passing the tiny Gwynne Street on your left.* Once
known as Pipewell Lane, a house, long since demolished, is believed
to have been where Nell Gwynne was born in humble circumstances.
As is well known, Nell went to London and started her career in the
capital by selling oranges. We may assume that she must have been
a striking woman for she attracted the roving eye of Charles II,
becoming one of his several mistresses, and providing him with two
sons. Long after she had exchanged Pipewell for Drury Lane the
Hereford connection was re-established when her grandson, James
Beauclerk, was installed as bishop in 1746.

*Continue to cross the Wye bridge, pausing to peer over the parapet
where quite large fish may be seen: carp, or perhaps a salmon, and
unhappily a supermarket trolley or two. Turn left along the riverside path
through the park with a fine view of the cathedral.* It is a scene set off by
the handsome copper beech and willows that bend to add their tears
to the river's flow or in vanity to admire their reflections in the clear
water. Beyond the cathedral a tall column, topped by a Grecian urn,

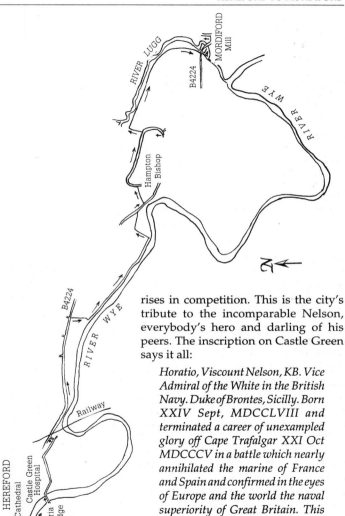

rises in competition. This is the city's tribute to the incomparable Nelson, everybody's hero and darling of his peers. The inscription on Castle Green says it all:

Horatio, Viscount Nelson, KB. Vice Admiral of the White in the British Navy. Duke of Brontes, Sicilly. Born XXIV Sept, MDCCLVIII and terminated a career of unexampled glory off Cape Trafalgar XXI Oct MDCCCV in a battle which nearly annihilated the marine of France and Spain and confirmed in the eyes of Europe and the world the naval superiority of Great Britain. This gallant hero captured or destroyed

107

47 ships of the line, in various engagements of enemies of his country. His fellow citizens of Hereford in grateful recognition of such pre-eminent services consecrate this column to his honoured and immortal memory MDCCCIX.

He was not neglected by the city during his lifetime for six years earlier he had been presented with the freedom of the city.

Soon Victoria Bridge is met and crossed. This was built entirely from money raised by voluntary subscriptions to mark the 60th year of the queen's reign in 1897 and prompts the thought that fund raising does not seem to have been a problem in Hereford when a popular celebration was in prospect.

From the bridge go forward and in a short distance turn right into Nelson Street, passing the hospital on your right. Continue down Harold Street and, on meeting Park Street, turn left to join the main road, the B4224. Turn right and follow it for nearly a mile. Quite soon the Salmon Inn is passed with its handsome sign - good enough to illustrate those fishermen's tales of "the one that got away".

At last, when you are beginning to wonder if you have missed your turning or have been condemned to an excess of road walking, the path to the riverside appears on your right, just opposite Sudbury Avenue. Take the path, go diagonally left and in 200 yards cross a stile and then go diagonally right to the river where you turn left and follow the path downstream.

The signal that the town has been left behind may be announced by the sudden flutter of a heron rising in a small commotion. A little island in the river had provided a nesting site for a pair of swans when I walked this way last. The nest was only a bare foot above the water level which seemed less than prudent, bearing in mind the exceptional winter floods that had only so recently subsided. Did the swans know something I didn't - and the arrangements they had made for accommodating their family were a reliable indication of another long dry summer? The answer was a definite "yes" as river levels fell and hosepipe bans were daily announced in successive areas of the country.

Follow the riverside, crossing the bottom edge of four fields, with the Herefordshire orchards away to your left, bright with white and pink blossom in May and later rich with fruit. The county is famous for its dairy farming and Friesian and Hereford cattle are likely to be seen in the meadows on both banks of the river.

At the end of the fourth field, cross a stile and swing left over a field as signed to cross a stream and further stile. In a few yards turn right on the path carried on a causeway, The Stank. In about 200 yards cross a stile and turn left to descend to the road and turn right.

Just beyond the telephone box turn left over a ditch and stile to cross a field towards bungalows seen ahead. Cross a further stile to meet a lane in 40 yards at the edge of Hampton Bishop and turn left. The lane is followed for about half a mile until it makes a junction with Church Lane, a quiet road with modern brick and tile giving way to the occasional thatch and half timber. Our route does not pass the little church of Saint Andrews but a diversion will reveal another cool and peaceful oasis and a welcome that reads:

> *This church does open stand*
> *That thou may sit, rest, think and pray,*
> *Remember whence thou art and what shall be thy end*
> *Remember us and go thy way in peace.*

Its long list of rectors starts with Henry de Shoreham who is dated uncertainly to a time prior to 1283. The arms of George III, 1791, are preserved upon the walls and there is a long list of benefactions. These include:

> *1823 The Rev Henry Huntington, the rector of this parish presented a handsome barrel organ for the use of the church.*
> *1694 Mr Thos Burge gave a bell to the church*
> *1793 Mr Freen, with the consent of the parish took into the Court Farm a piece of Common land for which he is to pay annually on Easter Monday £3 to the overseers of the poor.*

At the bend that marks the junction of Rectory Road with Church Lane turn left along a gravel lane and at the top take the path over a stile on the right. After a short passage between hedges, or in it, as it sometimes appears, emerge to go forward on a dirt lane on top of a causeway built above the flood plain of the River Lugg. The Lugg is a haunt of the kingfisher and the meadows are popular with swans; I was told of thirty-nine being counted grazing during the early spring.

Continue with the causeway through a succession of metal gates, at the end of the bank swinging right to meet a stile which gives access to the road over Mordiford bridge and turning left to reach the village.

16: Mordiford

Today Mordiford is as quiet and peaceful a place as you are likely to meet in a long day's march, with the River Lugg sparkling over its gravel bed as it hastens to consummate its marriage with the Wye.

It was not always, indeed is not always, so idyllic, as any riverside dweller will testify. Take the year of 1811, for instance. All manner of things were happening in the big, wide world. Arthur Wellesley, not yet Duke of Wellington but writing his name large in the history books, had evicted the French from Portugal and went on to victories in Spain. Jane Austen's Sense and Sensibility made its appearance on the literary scene and Macadam was in the early stages of his work that was to revolutionise the roads of Britain. But in Mordiford's small world this was the year of the great storm.

In one of those fits of temporary insanity that nature occasionally assumes to remind us how powerful she is and how weak we are the very hills trembled for four violent hours as a fearsome storm burst upon the village. Thunder pealed, incessantly echoing along the valley; great black clouds driven by a raging wind turned the May afternoon into a black night riven by forked lightning. And it rained like it had never rained before, not heaven's kindly benison but an assault upon the landscape that threatened to batter the world to pieces by its very power.

Many must have wondered if the day of judgment had come with the ungodly reviewing their lives and in fear turning uncharacteristically to prayer.

The tiny River Pentalow, in calmer times just a trickle and easily jumped by the village boys, found itself turned into an Amazon for the space of a few hours. Its breadth spread to 180 feet, its modest depth multiplied amazingly to 20 feet. It swept through the village as if possessed by the Devil, a wild thing contemptuously pushing aside anything that dared to bar its passage. A great barn was carried before it, a cider mill and the cottage next to it were treated with the same scant respect. The miller, William Husband, his niece

Ann Edwards, a widow, Elizabeth Greenly, and her young child Jemina were all drowned. Above the village hundreds of tons of rock were brought down and carried through the village by the torrent, causing many injuries and great damage to houses and sweeping away the gardens. The story was recorded by the then rector, Chas John Bird, who added that when the storm subsided an appeal for the relief of those who had suffered most raised £80 to alleviate their distress.

Until early in the nineteenth century the church was strangely adorned by a large green dragon painted on its western exterior wall, a not uncommon heraldic device which in this case was supposed to recall the times of earlier troubles which had descended upon the people of Mordiford - troubles which to the modern ear are rather less believable than the almighty storm which so devastated the village on the evening of May 27, 1811. It reads rather more like a fairy story and is perhaps best related in that style - thus:

Once upon a time, long, long ago, (when knights were not as bold as they have sometimes been made out), the village of Mordiford dwelt in fear of a dragon. From time to time the firey creature descended from his lair in the wooded hills to prey upon the cattle in the meadows. Serious as the loss of a valuable cow was, even worse was to follow as the dragon with increasing boldness carried off those who were responsible for tending the herd.

The news that the dragon was coming sent the villagers running in terror to hide in their houses until it was judged safe enough to emerge with dread in their hearts to discover the latest depredations. The dragon was the only topic of conversation and all attempts to trap the scaly creature were to no avail and sometimes ended in yet another tragedy. Increasingly valuable inducements were offered to anyone who would come forward to rid the village of the dragon but no one could be found who was sufficiently bold, resourceful or plain foolhardy enough to be tempted by the promised rewards.

The dragon continued his destructive way of life; more cattle went to assuage his increasing appetite and the villagers despaired of ever ridding themselves of the fearsome creature. At last someone reasoned that a man already condemned to death, and thus with nothing to lose, might be persuaded to take his chance with the dragon rather than the executioner. Such a convicted criminal was

111

at last found and agreed to the pardon terms offered in exchange for the death of the dragon.

Accordingly, the prisoner, whose name we do not know, gave great thought to the destruction of the dragon and the preservation of his own life, predating by many a century the great Doctor Johnson's assertion that when a man knows that he is to be hanged in a fortnight it concentrates his mind wonderfully. And so it did. The plan that he evolved, like all good plans, was simple.

Our hero, and hero he certainly was, despite his former misdemeanours, elected to hide in a barrel close to the river where the dragon was accustomed to drink. Thus it was that he was able to get close enough to kill the dragon.

The story should have had a happy ending for Mordiford's answer to Saint George, but alas the plans of mice and dragon slayers are apt to go astray. Having loosed off the fatal arrow from the security of his hide-out he gave away his presence by an injudiciously premature survey of the field of battle. Thus in the moment that he had achieved his freedom it was snatched away from him by the last dying firey breath of the dragon.

As I understand it, life is a little quieter at Mordiford these days.

17: Mordiford to How Caple

DISTANCE:	6^1/$_2$ miles approx.
DETAIL:	Lanes, field paths, and woodland with some fine views and orchids in season.
MAPS:	1:25,000 Pathfinder 1040 (SO 43/53) and (edge of) 1041 (SO 63/73). 1:50,000 Landranger 149
ACCOMMODATION:	Fownhope - but check for latest information from Hereford or Ross-on-Wye tourist offices.
SHOPS:	Village shop at Mordiford.
TOURIST INFORMATION:	St Owens Street, Hereford. HR1 2PJ (0432 268430)

Shortly after passing the church take the narrow lane on the right close to the post office. After crossing the bridge over the Pentaloe Brook bear left and in 200 yards meet and cross a minor road - the B4224. Go forward through the grounds of the mill to pass through a metal gateway and take the track forward.

Once over the stream continue through a short field with a hedge on your right to meet and cross a stile. Bear right over a stream and go forward through an orchard with a hedge on your right. At the top of the orchard cross a stile and make your way uphill on a hedged path soon to meet a lane. Go forward to pass Bagpipers Cottage on your right and on to Hope Springs Farm which is reached in about 300 yards.

Turn right to pass through the farmyard with its cats, dogs that do not bark at passers-by and free range chickens contentedly picking their way about the yard. Follow the farm track roughly southwards for 700 yards and when this swings sharp right, leave it to continue to a five-barred gate, found opposite a brick and stone cottage.

Maintain your direction to follow a field path for a little over half a mile. When an angle of hedge is met continue forward with the hedge to your left, soon to pass through a five-barred gate, cross a stream and meet a road. (If pursued south-westerly it will bring you to Fownhope in half a mile.)

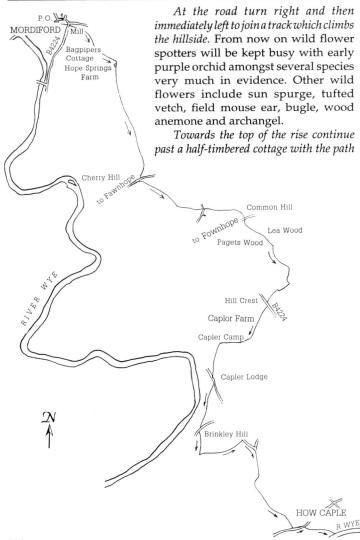

At the road turn right and then immediately left to join a track which climbs the hillside. From now on wild flower spotters will be kept busy with early purple orchid amongst several species very much in evidence. Other wild flowers include sun spurge, tufted vetch, field mouse ear, bugle, wood anemone and archangel.

Towards the top of the rise continue past a half-timbered cottage with the path soon climbing once more. When the path divides, ignore the right fork and continue forward into woods on a clear 'causewayed' path with a sharp fall on each side, again with further orchids. Views open up of the fine, beautifully rolling countryside with hedgerows white with May blossom and the landscape vividly splashed with oilseed rape in season.

On reaching a house continue forward along a track with more orchids to be seen in the ditch to your left, lady's smock alongside the lane, and more distantly farms set in the beautiful green landscape which is such an envied feature of the best English countryside.

Continue on past a large, white house with the legend REW 1840 set in the wall and in about 200 yards cross a rough lane and go forward uphill to join a grassy track. Cowslips are amongst the wild flowers found along the path edge. These old ways, often running between hedges, have become botanical nature reserves, often the only place you may see the wild flowers that were once such a common feature of the meadowlands. At one time the way was wide enough for it to have been a green lane, but the growth on either side of the hedges now confines the walker to a narrower tread.

When the path divides, go forward to cross a stile to climb to a wooded section announced by birch trees. At the top of a short flight of steps turn immediately left where a seat commands a fine view with the hills rolling westwards towards the not so distant Wales. The steeple of Fownhope church is seen half-right with a glimpse of the Wye beyond, a blue-grey artery set in a countryside of many shades of green; not exclusively so, for the painter of this broad canvas has varied and brightened it with white splashes of blossom in hedgerow and orchard, vivid, unnatural yellow of oilseed rape and, here and there, the dark reddy brown of a field not yet greened beneath which must be concealed main crop potatoes.

Continue between the trees, with the deep cleft of an old quarry, long since reclaimed by nature, to your right. On reaching a stile opposite a reservoir, cross, and turn left on a falling path to join a metalled track to meet a lane with Common Hill farm on your right.

Cross the lane to the stile opposite following a path downhill with a fence on your left, and soon swing left. In 100 yards cross a stile to enter Lea and Paget's Woods, a reserve of the Herefordshire Nature Reserve Trust and a sheltered habitat where the birds sing joyously. A gently rising path is pursued for about 400 yards until a crossing path is met by a bridle-

path sign and post with a reserve map and nature notes. The notes tell of rather more orchids than you may have identified: early purple, common twayblade, greater butterfly and common spotted. The ubiquitous bluebell is here, a great perfumed blue carpet hazing away into the deep recesses of the wood with here and there the purple of the orchids to be seen.

From the nature reserve post swing half-right to reach the edge of the wood in 200 yards and leave by way of a stile entwined with wild hops. Go forward with a hedge on your right, to meet a stile by a metal gateway and again continue, losing height. Cross a stile at the bottom corner of a field and follow the line of the fence to a stile opposite. Once over this swing right and at the bottom of the field pass through a metal gateway and turn left with a stream and hedge to your left. At the far side of the field turn uphill to the top corner of the field. Turn right here and in a few yards left over a stile. Turn right along the field edge for a few yards, then left to follow the long side of the field with a hedge on your right to meet a farm track.

Turn left with the track to meet the road just below Hill Crest Cottage. Turn left down the road and in about 90 paces turn right on a metalled lane towards Caplor Farm. In 200 yards, a little short of the farm, turn left over a stile and go forward along a field edge. In a few yards cross a stile on your right and go forward with a hedge and farm buildings on your right. Continue through a broken hedge and go forward through the next field to enter a wooded section where a stepped path assists progress to a stile to emerge into an open field.

Go forward, and as you top a short rise, make for the barn seen ahead and pass this on your left, then swing right to follow the bank of Capler Camp, a narrow oval-shaped earthwork, some 700 yards in length and now partly wooded. Its banks are bright with gorse and broom and offer fine views. To the left is the tree-crowned May Hill, a prominent landmark recognised by walkers from many points of the compass, the black, high ground of the Forest of Dean and a wide arc of numberless, and from this distance largely nameless, hills.

At the end of the bank, cross a stile into woodland bordered by two great oaks, and go forward. Soon the path emerges into the open; here turn left over a stile and make your way diagonally right through a fir plantation. At the bottom edge meet and cross a stile, turning left to enter Capler Wood on a wide track where campion and herb robert may be added to the wild flower collection.

Capler Camp

On reaching the lane, turn left past Capler Lodge with a sudden delightful glimpse of the Wye far below. In 50 yards turn right on a track and pursue this for a little under half a mile to reach the road at Brinkley Hill. Cross the road and take the track diagonally opposite, and in a quarter of a mile turn sharp left along a hedged lane to meet a road in 750 yards. Turn right and follow this for 600 yards to reach Totnor. Just after passing Llanstephan House on your left, take the track on the right, found through a metal gateway which soon descends over field to meet and cross a stream by a sturdy footbridge.

Here turn left and follow a path along a fence line which eventually decants onto a wide track running between a hedge and trees to meet a lane at the edge of How Caple. The house to your left was once a mill, but was converted to a private residence in 1904. A pair of cannons defends the front door, which are believed to have done duty at the Battle of Killiecrankie in 1689, thus making them over 300 years old.

Turn left along the lane, passing a telephone box and crossing a stream to continue with the Wye Valley Walk route on your right.

117

18: How Caple to Ross-on-Wye

DISTANCE:	5¹/₂ miles approx.
DETAIL:	Mainly level walking on field paths and quiet lanes finishing with the classic view of Ross-on-Wye.
MAPS:	1:25,000 - SO 63/73 (1041) edge of: SO 62/72 (Pathfinder 1065), Pathfinder 1064 (SO 42/52)
	1:50,000 Landranger 149 & 162
ACCOMMODATION:	Ross-on-Wye.
TOILETS:	Ross-on-Wye.
SHOPS:	Ross-on-Wye.
TOURIST INFORMATION:	Wyedean Tourist Board, 20 Broad Street, Ross-on-Wye. HR9 7EA (0989 62768)

How Caple is a tiny village, a scatter of houses with a hilltop church which the walker may glimpse through the trees from the river bank. Sharing the hilltop is How Caple Court, which in over 800 years has been home to only three families: Caple, Gregory and Lee. Those who make a diversion from the route to visit the church will find a quiet, cool haven from the heat of a summer day and, aided by the leaflet, a story of centuries of care that is so often demonstrated in our village churches. The keys can be obtained from the nearby fabric shop in the courtyard by the garden centre.

We have already paid our respect at the shrine of St Thomas Cantilupe in Hereford Cathedral where he was bishop in the thirteenth century. How does a bishop's name find its way into the calendar of saints and, in particular, what led to the canonisation of Thomas some forty years after his death? We know that Thomas was a scholarly man, professor and later Chancellor of Oxford University: a man involved in the politics of the day but with a care for the parishes under his charge, a man who walked with the great of the land, but lived simply and earned the regard of the poor. Such was his reputation that following his death miracles, numbered in hundreds, were claimed by those who made intercessions at his tomb.

One such event is associated with How Caple where, some years after the death of the goodly Thomas, a child fell in the river. Rescue came too late and it was a lifeless body that was recovered from the water. The grief-wracked family could not revive him but in one last act of desperation lit a candle to Thomas. Remarkably the child recovered, the victim of the unrelenting waters of the Wye snatched back from beyond the jaws of death by the light of a flickering candle and the faith of the family in the power of a goodly man whose body had been laid to rest in the cathedral nearly twenty years earlier - an incredible story but not one standing alone, just one of dozens of stories of the apparently dead being restored to their families.

The Route

Having followed this section of the Wye Valley Walk in late April, I tend to think of this in terms of colour - the yellow and blue walk. The yellow is provided by the blazing luminescence of a great field of oilseed rape and the blue by the masses of bluebells running up the wooded hillsides. Both in themselves are common enough sights to the country goer nevertheless they always provide moments of visual and aromatic pleasure as each spring comes round.

Picking up the way from the last stage, the lane at the edge of How Caple is reached by a house noted for its unusual security measures, a pair of ancient cannons that guards the front door. Turn left along the lane to cross a stream and take the signed path on the right to follow a field edge with the stream in its deep ditch to your right, noisy with the sound of geese. Pursue the path to reach the Wye in a little over a quarter of a mile. Absence makes the heart grow fonder they say, and certainly it is a very welcome pleasure to again be in close company with the river after several miles of separation. *Turn left heading downstream, as it runs rippling and sparkling over the rapids with the occasional clump of pink campion brightening the grassy banks. Now follow the bank side for just over half a mile with How Caple church briefly, almost shyly, appearing from behind the trees.*

As the river starts yet another of its loops, cross a stile and turn immediately left up a grassy bank to reach a narrow road in 50 yards and

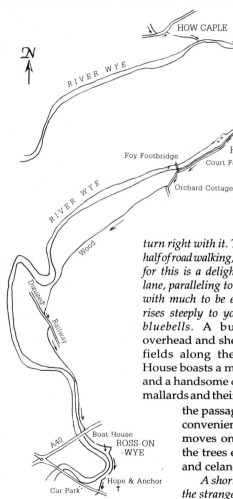

turn right with it. There is now a mile and half of road walking, but suppress the groans for this is a delightful, pleasant country lane, paralleling to the course of the river, with much to be enjoyed. Lyndor Wood rises steeply to your left, carpeted with bluebells. A buzzard soars high overhead and sheep take their ease in fields along the riverside. Lyndor House boasts a millstone in its garden and a handsome copper beech. Gaudy mallards and their dowdy wives watch the passage of the river from a convenient rock and our way moves on under the shade of the trees edged with bluebells and celandine.

A short climb takes the lane to the strangely named Hole-in-the-Wall with its adventure activity centre. Colourful canoes lie upturned on the banks awaiting the arrival of the young adventurers who will take the passage downstream to Ross-on-Wye. A stone house bears the legend, "John Abrahall 1640". He built simply but well in materials that were made to last.

Nearly half a mile beyond Hole-in-the-Wall Foy Bridge is reached but not crossed, although few will resist the opportunity to pause and use it as a viewpoint to survey the river.

Beyond the bridge the lane begins to pull away from the Wye and in about 300 yards, opposite Orchard Cottage, take the path on the right which runs through a small plantation with the little settlement and church of Foy seen across the river.

A short passage along the fenced path leads into a field; here go forward to meet a wide track which is followed to the end of the field to reach a metal gate. Once through the gateway continue with a hedge on your right. The track peters out but maintain your direction to the end of the field to enter a wood by a stile. In late April this little stretch of woodland, Monks Grove, may prove to be the most rewarding part of this section of the walk, for bluebells are thickly massed, crowding up to the edges of the path so that you must have a care where you place your feet. A heady perfume hangs in the air and the more open aspect offers better photographic opportunities.

Ignore the path that appears on the right shortly after entering the wood and continue through the length of the wood close to its edge, passing a sandstone quarry face, and you may wonder if this once formed the bank of a wider river. Exit from the woods by a small flight of steps to a stile which gives onto a field, probably to be found under crops. Take the path facing the stile and in 125 paces turn left to follow the path along hedgerow which is kept to your right.

At the end of the field cross a stile and turn right along a track with the Wye looping off to the right. Upstream will be seen the remains of the supports that once carried the railway over the Wye - Atlas without his burden. In 100 yards pass through a metal gateway, and go forward along a field edge with a fence on your left, having left the Wye to find its own, and for the moment separate, way to Ross. At the bottom of the field, cross a stile and mount steps to the former railway embankment and turn left along the old track. It sits a little above the fields, the engineers no doubt needing to keep the track above flood level. After a while the track enters a cutting with holes in the bank that suggests something bigger than rabbits

121

and mice live here - perhaps a fox or badgers.

As progress is made the spire of Ross's church comes into view, framed by the trees and behind it the backcloth of the high wooded hills beyond the town which are climbed in the next section of this walk.

When the track merges into open fields, turn sharp right and in about 50 yards left to follow the river bank with a hedge coming between you and the river at first. Continue with the riverside path to pass under the modern bridge carrying the A40 with the classic prospect of Ross-on-Wye becoming increasingly prominent - the tall graceful spire of the church, the white Royal Hotel beneath it keeping company with the sham gothic tower.

When the rowing club premises are reached bear to the left, passing through a kissing gate and over a stream to follow the fence line and on to a second kissing gate and bridge. Continue forward to join and follow the river bank along the parkland given by John Kyrle to the town. The houses of Ross, white, green and pink, rise up the hillside while willows dip low over the river and you may catch the electric blue flash of a kingfisher flying fast and low over the water.

The path passes through the gardens of the Hope and Anchor, the second part of the name clearly demonstrated in the grounds whilst I suppose the hope expresses the wish that they will still be open by the time you arrive. There is an ice cream kiosk close at hand, other refreshments at the Riverside Restaurant and toilets just beyond.

Those seeking accommodation or set to explore the town should now turn left and head up the hill. If you are continuing your journey, or picking up the route after your tour of inspection head diagonally across the greensward and cross the road to continue on to the twin arched underpass to the car park where the next section of the walk begins.

19: Ross-on-Wye

The old-time traveller trudging a dusty way might have been expected to have experienced a tingle of excitement as the next town on his journey came into view. Here was a chance of refreshment, to renew his meagre supplies, to catch up with the latest news, a welcome place of safety perhaps, the certainty of a good night's sleep, or simply another stage in a journey that he had perforce to take on foot, completed. Today most of us who travel on foot do so by choice, electing to do so for the pleasant but not over aggressive exercise it offers, a chance to enjoy the many pleasures of the countryside, a self-set voyage of discovery with its own mild adventures. Nevertheless something of that excitement engendered in the traveller of old is likely to be shared by the modern day pilgrim as towards the end of the day he is afforded a glimpse of his next port of call.

Ross-on-Wye is just such a place, its presence first heralded by the slender, needle-like spire of the parish church. Steadily the details of the scene are painted in, as the town comes more prominently into the view - a town rising sharply from the river providing an almost continental touch, the white walls of the Royal Hotel reflecting back the light of the sun, the pastel colour washes of lesser houses adding variety to the palette. Closer inspection reveals the darker, grimmer tones of a tower, like the town walls, a sham built in 1833 during the construction of Wilton Road, a piece of civic vanity. Close by is the solid building of the British and Foreign Schools, again mildly suggestive of a continental connection. The society was formed in 1808 anxious to promote education which was so sadly lacking. A plaque on the wall passes on the information that the school was "established 1837 to educate children from different backgrounds".

Ross is a busy, bustling little market town and gives the impression that it has long been so. Its narrow streets make Saturday morning a minor nightmare and, atmosphere apart, it is best explored at a quieter time. Certainly it is accustomed to receiving the traveller as its inns so clearly demonstrate; Admiral Lord Nelson, at the

The Market Hall, Ross-on-Wye

height of his fame stopped at the Swan and Falcon in 1802, a sojourn anticipated by John Byng, the Fifth Viscount Torrington, author of the *Torrington Diaries,* who lodged here in 1787. The great Charles Dickens gave his patronage to the Royal Hotel when he was here in the early autumn of 1867. Samuel Taylor Coleridge, he of the *Rhyme of the Ancient Mariner* and *Kubla Khan,* opted for the King s Arms.

124

Clearly the Hope and Anchor catered for the river travellers, busy with the comings and goings of commercial traffic or seeing the Wye tourists off on the way downstream by boat eager to drink in the romance of travel as they dreamed their way down to the delights of Symonds Yat, Tintern Abbey and Chepstow Castle. The King's Head, its sign carrying the portrait of Charles II, was a posting inn, speeding the mail with a change of horses. The streets of Ross must have echoed to the thrilling call of the post horn announcing the pending arrival of the mail, warning the ostlers to have the change of horses at the ready or commanding the keeper at the toll house to fling wide his gates and not delay his majesty's mail - an exciting concept still a popular subject of Christmas cards.

It is whilst we are on the subject of inns that we take up the story of the town's most famous citizen, John Kyrle, now well remembered as the Man of Ross, with an inn, probably uniquely, dedicated to his name in Wye street, where it proudly carries not one but two portraits upon its white frontage. The visitor encounters, knowingly or not, echoes of John Kyrle almost everywhere he goes. Although not born in Ross he clearly adopted it as his own, becoming its great benefactor of the seventeenth century, scattering his goodwill in many directions, feeding the poor, caring for the sick, arranging for fresh water and promoting the cause of education. His handsome, half-timbered jettied house, now shops, stands close to the market hall and, like the inn named after him, carries his portrait and the date of his death, November 7, 1724. The market hall has a story connected with Kyrle, who was an ardent Royalist. A bust of Charles II had been erected on the market house out of sight of the Man of Ross. This displeased the town's leading citizen who felt that he too should be afforded the pleasure of paying his respects to the monarch. Accordingly he paid for a further portrait of the king to be installed on the building within sight of his windows. It is still there today and the letters F C can be discerned, Kyrle's own expression of loyalty - "Faithfull to Charles in Heart".

His sixty-four years as a resident of the town are marked by one act of generosity after another. We owe the graceful tall spire of Saint Mary's Church, a landmark for many miles to his beneficence; when a new bell was needed he was on hand to pay for it. The viewpoint close to the church, The Prospect, was a present to the town. It could scarcely have been better named for surely from here every prospect pleases, with the fine view of the river's winding course through the green meadows enjoyed to the full.

John Kyrle was not the town's only benefactor; the almshouses in Church Street were repaired by William Rudhall in 1575. They are still there today, serving the needs of the elderly. The first premises must have been on the cramped side, for in 1960 the original fifteen houses were converted to three, the work being accomplished without altering the Tudor frontage. In the churchyard a white monument topped by a Grecian urn commemorates Walter Scott, who died in 1786, "the grateful restorer of the Blue Coat School". Yet another resident of the town, James Baker, a local boy who left to seek his fortune in London did not forget the place of his birth. The inscription on his tomb in the churchyard says it all:

In memory of James Baker of London, a native of this town who died 24th June 1836 aged 72. By his will dated 5th November 1835 he left upwards of twenty thousand pounds to the poor inhabitants of this parish, the interest thereof to be distributed twice in the year or oftener by the churchwardens and overseers of the parish in clothing, food and fuel to such as do not receive alms of the said parish for ever, preference being always given to those poor persons born in this parish. In his youth he experienced poverty and neglect but by great industry he provided a goodly proportion for the poor of this parish for many ages and for himself an imperishable name which will be repeated with feeling of gratitude when those of the scornful oppressors of mankind shall be forgotten or remembered only to be execrated.

It sounds a friendly, caring welcoming place, for centuries gathering to itself the farmer bringing his produce to market, the people of the outlying countryside coming into shop, providing rest for the traveller and facilitating the speedy passage of the mail. All in fact that you might expect from a small country market town.

It was not always so, for time was when the town had to put up the shutters and retire within itself; the bridge, once the gateway to the town, became a barrier. Outsiders were no longer welcome, nor for that matter did they wish to come to Ross. For in the fateful year of 1637 the plague reached Ross, brought in perhaps by a traveller

The Plague Cross, Ross-on-Wye

from London, where it had been rife the previous year. The Black Death, much dreaded, had stretched out its long arm to seize the people of Ross. Many people fled the town hoping to escape its

127

fearsome clutches. The bridge marked a point beyond which no man would pass, and supplies being brought to the town were left here to be collected with payment being left in a pot of vinegar.

The plague raged, claiming victim after victim until it became a never-ending nightmare. A great pit was dug in the churchyard and the dead were brought from their houses and buried without the benefit of a coffin, although the vicar courageously remained to commit their souls to the healing hands of God. In all, 315 people fell victim to the disease and are remembered by the Plague Cross erected close to the pit where they still lie today.

All visitors to Ross will be drawn to Saint Mary's Church, which incidentally has one of the best kept churchyards you are likely to see. Notably there is a children's section, heart rending but rich with the flowers of remembrance. I recall clearly visiting it close to the Easter season and noting that there was scarcely a grave in the whole of the churchyard that did not have fresh flowers upon it.

Much history is reflected in the brief lines of memorials in churches like that in Ross. The story of men of action who joined the services such as John Thirkell of the 88th Connaught Rangers ..."who died near Stangar in Natal, 22nd April, 1879 from the effects of fever contracted while on active service in Zulu land". Men of industry like John Partridge..."native of this town where his family long resided, who in the pursuit of the iron trade occasioned him in early life to remove to Monmouth where he continued to in death, he always retained for the place of his birth a fond attachment. He was ever ready to evince in the promotion of objects of public utility and in what was more congenial to the unobtrusive modesty and benevolence of his deportment in acts of private charity".

John Kyrle is of course remembered with a monument in the chancel but more unusually in "his trees". His accustomed seat in the church was immediately under a window, where some time after his death two elm shoots pushed their way up through the floor close to his pew. Clearly this was an omen, and the intrusive tree should not be cut back.

Nature took its usual course and the trees died but the damage caused by their invasion let in the joint scourges of woodworm and dry rot so that the floor had to be replaced. Tradition dies hard, the trees were a nice thought and a totally suitable remembrance of the

Above:
Wye Valley from
Yat Rock

Right:
Canoeists under
instruction.
Symonds Yat

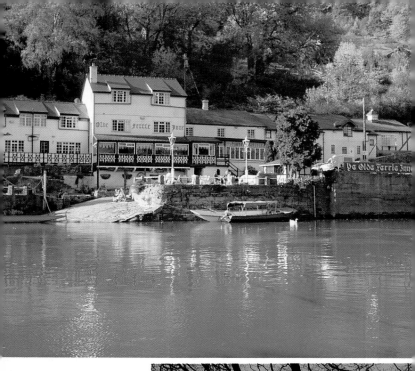

Above:
Old Ferrie Inn
Symonds Yat
west from the river

Right:
Kymin Tower
(possible diversion)

town's great friend so that two creepers were planted in a trough and continue there today.

There is a group of memorials honouring the Rudhall family, William Rudhall, who died in 1530, and his wife Anne. He held the post of Attorney General to Arthur, Prince of Wales. Another William Rudhall who died in 1609 is believed to have founded the almshouses that carry the family name. There is a splendid table tomb to John Rudhall, with his wife Mary, with their children depicted around the base, including some who pre-deceased them carrying skulls - a somewhat grisly monumental convention.

Most striking of all is the fine statue of a man clad in Roman armour and equipped with sword and shield - not a centurion, but certainly a fighting man - Colonel William Rudhall who died in 1651. He recalls another time during the Civil War when some "visitors" to Ross were not welcome and the bridge again was used in an attempt to deny entry to the town. A supporter of the Royalist cause he led his troops, albeit unsuccessfully, into the fray at Wilton Bridge. (The walk does not quite reach the bridge, but there is an old sun dial set on a column although the inscription is now unreadable - time perhaps for a little restoration work? On the other bank are the remains of Wilton Castle.)

We too, like the travellers of the past, must move on but there is much to remember about Ross when the journey down the Wye is done: the busy market hall which has seen its traders and customers gather about its steps down the centuries, the graceful spire of the church, but perhaps above all, the picture of Ross in its hour of greatest need, when the townsfolk under the leadership of their faithful vicar processed through the streets chanting the litany in a plea for deliverance from the pestilence that was upon them.

20: Ross-on-Wye to Kerne Bridge
(with extension to Goodrich Castle)

DISTANCE:	5¼ miles.
DETAIL:	The river is deserted for a pleasant if slightly strenuous switchback route over wooded heights.
MAPS:	Inconveniently spread over several:
	1:25,000 Pathfinder 1064 (SO 42/52) SO 62/72 (Pathfinder 1065) and Outdoor Leisure No.14 - The Wye Valley. Otherwise use the 1:50,000 Landranger Sheet 162.
ACCOMMODATION:	Ross-on-Wye. Goodrich.
TOILETS:	Ross-on-Wye and Goodrich Picnic Site.
SHOPS:	Ross-on-Wye and Goodrich.
TOURIST INFORMATION:	Wyedean Tourist Board, 20 Broad Street, Ross-on-Wye. HR9 7EA (0989 62768)

This section of the walk starts from the Wilton Road car park which is found from the riverside by passing under the road by the arched underpass. Those exploring the town may pick up the route at Alton Road.

From the southern side of the underpass go forward through the end of the car park to cross a bridge over a small stream. Head up the bank, at the top veering half-left and in a few yards swinging right on a wider track with a row of Scots pines making a one-sided guard of honour. Not, however, for the benefit of the Wye Valley walker for in a few yards you turn left through a kissing gate to take the fenced path close to the sports field.

Exit from a further kissing gate and bear right at Rectory Farm to follow the lane with the graceful spire of the parish church seen to your left. Continue to meet the B4228 road and turn left with it. After passing the Saint Francis of Rome RC Church turn right along Alton Street where there is a Victorian letterbox set in the wall. The road climbs, with the wooded slopes of Penyard Park seen ahead as you top the rise and descend again.

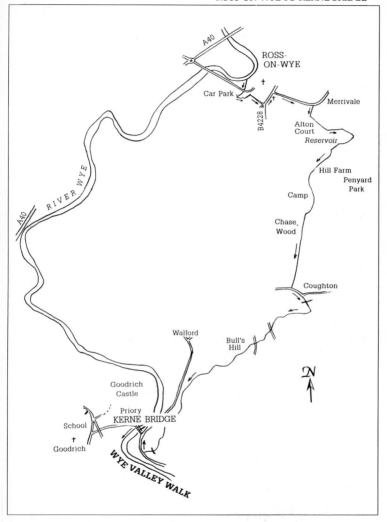

At the foot of the hill, as the road swings to the left, turn right along Penyard Lane. After passing the handsome "black and white" tall timber-framed building with mullion windows and a beautifully tiled roof - Alton Court - go forward between trees on the footpath signed to Penyard.

Exit from the wooded section into an open field and continue with the rising path with a hedge on your left. The path curves to the right following the outside edge of a wood. After passing a covered reservoir on your right the path plunges into woods for a short spell. On emerging into the open swing sharp right towards a farm gateway. There are fine views to Ross dominated by Saint Mary's Church. By a metal gate cross a stile to enter a wood and swing half-left.

After a modest climb on a pleasant path decorated in season with celandine and wood anemone leave the wood near the buildings of Hill Farm to join a track. After 100 yards swing left along the broad track with wooded Penyard Park across the valley to the east. The track rises through Chase Wood edging the eastern boundaries of yet another of the hill forts that are found successively down the Wye Valley.

Continue with the broad track until it divides at an "island". Ignore the broad tracks on the left and right and go forward to descend on a narrow path. After about a hundred yards swing sharp left, again on a narrow and steeply falling path. A crossing path is shortly reached; here turn left and immediately right to descend with the aid of steps.

As the wood edge is reached continue downhill on the inside of the wood which is left by a stile at a five-barred gate. Then take the field path passing under power lines to reach a minor road at Coughton after negotiating a succession of metal gates.

Turn left and follow the lane for about 200 yards, and as it starts to curve take the signed path on the right and make your way uphill with the field boundary on your left to meet a stile at the top of the field. Cross a lane and further stiles and go forward on a rising path through beech trees. After a short distance, as you draw level with the house to your right, swing left over a short field and turn right along a (at first) level track, passing the attractive Rose Cottage.

The path rises and, on meeting a rough lane, turn right and continue to meet a metalled lane. Cross a stile opposite and descend on a narrow path. After a short distance meet and cross a stile and bear right downhill soon to cross stream by a plank bridge. Climb again, over a field - slightly diagonally left - to meet a stile by a house, where a stepped path leads onto *a lane. Here turn left and cross the road immediately to take the path opposite signed to Walford which descends through a deep hollow way with a succession of beehives on both sides.*

This path is now pursued south-westerly along the edge of the wood, ignoring the turn to Walford seen below away to your right and, as progress is made, the neatly stacked planks and logs of the distant timber yard. The path leads onto the road, but not quite, for just short of it turn left up a track with a cottage wall to your left lined with wall pennywort, climbing with the seemingly long-lost river in view again after an absence of some miles.

Pass the attractive Cherry Tree Cottage, rising through the beech trees until a further cottage is met, still with its well and pump. Pass between two buildings; the house on the left is Oak Gables. A falling track is followed for about 200 yards before swinging right on a narrow path, continuing with it as it bears right to meet a lane. Here turn half-right, downhill, and when a large house is met, swing left down steps to meet the road by the Kerne Bridge Inn (bus stop and telephone).

Cross the road and swing right with the path to meet and cross Kerne Bridge.

Diversion to Goodrich Village and Castle

Continue up the road with the great bulk of Goodrich Castle seen on the hillside ahead half-right, soon passing Flanesford Priory, an Augustinian foundation established by Richard Talbot of Goodrich Castle in 1346. Fish was an important part of the diet and the monks, close as they were to the river, found it convenient to maintain fish ponds which can still be seen near the road.

At the top of the hill turn right, signed to Goodrich Castle, and at the school turn right again to the castle picnic site and car park (toilets and refreshments).

21: Goodrich Castle

Wye Valley explorers will probably get their first glimpse of Goodrich Castle as they climb the road from Kerne Bridge, a great but indeterminate stone block sitting heavily on the ridge. It disappears from view and is not seen again until, having passed through the country park, the walker emerges from the trees to meet it at close quarters - a majestic confrontation that may evoke an involuntary gasp of surprise.

Here is the very picture of defiance, a castle built out of the living rock, thrusting skyward from the deep moat from which the sandstone was quarried to construct the walls and towers. It is a very substantial ruin, sufficiently substantial for one to imagine a cheerful estate agent in the optimistic language of his profession describing it as: "a desirable listed property in red sandstone, having three floors, built between the twelfth and sixteenth century with commanding views over the River Wye and the Herefordshire countryside. Standing in its own grounds and not overlooked. In need of some renovation..."and so on.

The castle occupies a strong natural defensive position with the deep, dry moat adding to the sense of security which its residents must have felt even in the troubled centuries of its construction. It is a castle that presents two faces to the visitor. There is the obvious military aspect with its keep and great towers with their narrow windows and arrow slits - silent stones that speak volumes for the wealth and power of its various owners including the Earls of Pembroke and later the Earls of Shrewsbury, inheritors of the site first built on by Godric. But there is a quieter, gentler touch to be found here as well, evinced in the roofed chapel where the sun streams in through its leaded windows and little pools of colour lie upon the floor reflected from the centre panel of stained glass, far warmer and kinder than the dark narrow stone staircases where a man could hold an army at bay until his sword arm gave out.

The view from the castle is superb, the river far below with swans in slow, majestic procession. We may imagine the landscape much as it has been over the centuries save for the tiny bus crossing

Goodrich Castle

Kerne Bridge and the pylons of the national grid taking their giant strides across the countryside: the reddy-brown earth of the ploughed fields in harmony with the matured red sandstone of the castle, the distant spire of the church at Ross, and the older hill fort hidden away amongst the trees on Chase Hill.

In so romantic a setting such a castle as this must have a story to tell, a love story? Perhaps a ghost story? Goodrich, it seems, has both in one episode.

By the time of the English Civil War the castle was no longer occupied but its obvious strength ensured that it was soon drawn into the conflict, first being held by supporters of the Parliamentarian cause, then by the Royalists. It was a sad time, the country divided against itself, one man swearing his allegiance to King Charles I, the next avowing his support for Cromwell and Parliament. In 1646 the Royalist campaign was going badly and soon the king himself was to be forced into surrendering to the Scots at Newark. Goodrich was

135

under siege by troops under the command of Parliamentarian Colonel Birch and this is where our story begins. It seems that the colonel had a niece, by the name of Alice, who was in love with one of the defenders of the castle, Charles Clifford. A hopeless situation you may think, but love does not respect the boundaries imposed by kings or their soldiers and somehow Alice contrived to slip away and join Charles in the castle. They may have thought that their troubles were at an end, but in truth they were just beginning.

The pressure of the siege increased, artillery was brought into play and the water supply was running low. They were doubly in trouble, capture and separation seemed inevitable. An attempt at an escape was the only possible chance of happiness.

A black stormy night presented them with the possibility of getting away unseen; sentries taking cover from the rain would be less vigilant, the darkness would hide them and the noise of the storm would mask the sound of their horse. It worked, they got through the Parliamentarian lines without being spotted and full escape was only the width of the river away. Jordan to be passed and all would be well but the storm that had covered their escape was to prove their undoing; the river, volatile as ever, was in flood. There was no bridge to aid them on their way, nor would there be for a further 182 years, and to call out the ferryman was to ensure discovery. There was nothing for it but to press the horse forward, plunge into the dark waters, head downstream and hope the river would sweep them on to the opposite bank and safety. It was not to be; horse, man and maid drowned. Inevitably it is claimed that on similar nights of storm a mounted couple may be seen riding down to the river and disappearing in the torrent.

A sombre note on which to end the visit to Goodrich but the walker should be cheered by the thought that the next few miles will carry him into the Forest of Dean and to one of the finest viewpoints of the entire journey.

22: Kerne Bridge to Yat Rock

DISTANCE:	5¹/₄ miles.
DETAIL:	Level walking keeping close company with the river as the hills gradually close in to form the deep gorge, culminating in the famous view from Yat Rock.
MAPS:	Outdoor Leisure Map No.14 -The Wye Valley (1:25,000). Landranger Sheet 162
ACCOMMODATION:	Youth Hostel at Welsh Bicknor, hotels at Symonds Yat.
TOILETS:	Goodrich Castle picnic site, Yat Rock.
SHOPS:	Goodrich. Refreshments at Yat Rock in season.
TOURIST INFORMATION:	Wyedean Tourist Board, 20 Broad Street, Ross-on-Wye. HR9 7EA (0989 62768)

The Wye is famous for its great serpentine loops and this section of the walk leads to the best known meander as the river dives deep into the gorge cut beneath the high wooded limestone cliffs that dominate the scenery.

Join the riverside path on the western side of Kerne Bridge for five miles of relaxing level walking, a relief from the ups and downs of the last few miles. After following the edge of two fields cross a stile to continue with the riverside path under the shade of Thomas Wood for a mile. Keep an eye open for the blue flash that marks the speedy flight of a kingfisher, or the more lugubrious heron. Swans and mallards are certain to be seen as the river makes its way, chuckling over its stony bed.

Once free of the trees, continue on the grassy riverside path with Courtfields seen high to your right and Lydbrook coming into view on the opposite bank, its houses rising high up the hillside. A great patch of cowslips bursts forth and willows lean towards the water at a crazy angle, but somehow manage to maintain a foothold, their lower branches thick with the debris of the winter floods.

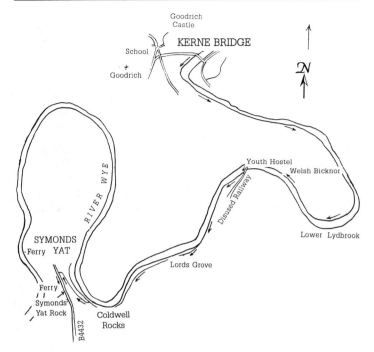

Soon we are at Welsh Bicknor, at the end of the no through road from Goodrich, and, despite its name, firmly in England. The little church, ensures its technical classification as a village, whilst the large rectory now does duty as a youth hostel. Notices along the river bank implore the adventurous to Keep off the Cribbes.

Continue past the youth hostel with the peace of the riverside unexpectedly broken by the noise of industry from the factory on the Lydbrook bank. When the former railway viaduct is met cross the river by the accompanying footbridge. On the far side descend steps to the left and pass under the bridge to take the path signed to Symonds Yat.

Pursue the river downstream after passing through a car park before joining the bankside path through fields. This is another well-fished stretch of the Wye with the chatter of the water competing with the

Welsh Bicknor, despite its name in Herefordshire

whirr of the factory. It was ever so along the lower Wye Valley, with the clangour of iron founding, the clunk of adze on wood in the boat yards resounding across the waters, and smoke from the furnaces billowing skyward, adding their glow to that of the setting sun.

139

Soon the wooded heights of Lords Grove are seen ahead and the walker may feel a little tingle of extra interest with the knowledge that the approach is being made to the deeply carved section of the river around Yat Rock. The hills gradually close in and as the river starts yet another sharp bend turn left to climb steps and turn right along the course of the old railway track.

The river temporarily disappears as the way goes through a shallow cutting, the temperature noticeably warmer in this sheltered area. In a little over quarter of a mile the path emerges into open fields again as the river curves towards Coldwell Rocks. Here the peregrines have returned to breed on the limestone bluffs thrust out from the thickly wooded cliffs.

The track moves into the woods again, this time with the temperature dropping under the shade of the trees and the cooling properties of the rocks. In half a mile a sign directs you left to Yat Rock. Take the narrow path which runs up the hillside with primroses, ramson, yellow archangel, wood anemones, and bird's nest fern creating a changing carpet on the rock-strewn forest floor.

In about quarter of a mile a further sign directs you left to Yat Rock on a path that zigzags uphill past a cottage to reach a minor road. Here turn left and after a short distance meet the Forestry Commission's car park and picnic site with access to the Yat Rock viewpoint.

23: Yat Rock

It is unlikely that you will be alone on Yat Rock, for from this lofty eyrie there is one of the finest and most photographed views in England. The river is seen to perfection as it pursues its course in the gorge beneath the steep, wooded cliffs. From the eastern side the visitor looks down upon the great, green canopy of the trees and the winding river. Over the river the rough and rocky brown slopes of Coppet Hill rise in direct contrast to the green pastures where diminutive cattle graze as in a toy farm yard. Looking north beyond Huntsham Hill the long rolling countryside of Herefordshire sweeps away into the blue of infinity.

Here the river makes yet another of its great loops, the most famous, as it sweeps round the hills taking a diversion of more than three miles to fill the gap which at its narrowest is little more than a quarter of a mile: a steadfast rocky fortress that all the waters of the Wye have not been able to wash away. Take a few steps to the western edge of this walled observation tower to look down once again as the Wye returns to divide the twin villages of Symonds Yat. The white houses of Symonds Yat West rise up the steep slopes of Great Doward in a forest that would serve well for a shade card of all the greens. Downstream there are glimpses of the white water of the rapids and beyond the continuing line of the cliffs with the bare rock thrusting out between the trees. Can this really be England? Have all those who rush abroad each year forgotten what they have on their doorstep?

In recent years there has been another attraction for the growing number of tourists who visit this corner of the Forest of Dean - the peregrines. Upstream, a third of a mile from the viewpoint, the sheer cliff of Coldwell Rocks has provided a safe breeding site for the birds which have returned to the forest after thirty years' absence. A safe breeding site is a relative term for it is made safe, not by the difficult access to the cliffs, but by the twenty-four hour watch mounted each year by the RSPB. Eggs and young birds command high prices and the unscrupulous have been known to steal both despite the protection afforded by law.

A peep at the peregrines

The peregrine is the mighty hunter of the air, going for the kill in a power dive that may accelerate up to 125 miles an hour. Food is plentiful here, wood pigeons and jackdaws ensuring that the young do not go hungry. The birds nest towards the end of March, laying three or four eggs which hatch after an incubation period of thirty-six days. The young birds fly after a month but stay with their parents until self sufficient when the parent birds drive them off to find hunting territories of their own. I make no pretensions to be a bird expert, or any other sort of expert for that matter, but I am told that the peregrines require a territory of 25 square miles. If true, it is surprising since wood pigeons are in abundance in many parts of the country, and those other cliff dwellers, jackdaws, are not in short supply.

The young birds do not come to full breeding maturity until they are about three years old but they seem to have a reasonably long life. With a minimum of disturbance and the watching brief of the RSPB we may expect to see an increase in breeding pairs as the effects of the pesticides which greatly reduced their numbers after the last war fade away. The pair that I watched from Yat Rock have returned to breed there for at least eight years, the female having been positively identified by a foot injury.

From spring onwards the RSPB's voluntary wardens provide watching facilities from Yat Rock and at weekends there is a steady queue of people eager to take a look at the birds through the high-powered telescopes.

It is not only the peregrines that can be watched from above; a few minutes spent looking up and down the river is likely to produce sightings of the graceful, soaring buzzard, the cormorants which frequent this stretch of the river, or a wide-winged heron.

It is a pleasure to view the landscape from this beautiful spot; it is a privilege to be able to walk into the landscape itself and we must be on our way.

24: Yat Rock to Monmouth

DISTANCE:	Via Wye Valley Walk: 7¹/₂ miles approx. using short cut: 6¹/₂ miles approx.
DETAIL:	A steep and scenic descent from Yat Rock to Symonds Yat East is followed by level walking to Monmouth.
MAPS:	1:25,000 Outdoor Leisure Map No.14 1:50,000 Landranger Sheet 162.
ACCOMMODATION:	Hotels at Symonds Yat but more general range at Monmouth..
TOILETS:	Yat Rock. Monmouth.
SHOPS:	Monmouth.
TOURIST INFORMATION:	Church Street, Monmouth, Gwent. NP5 3BK (0600 3899)

The continuation of the walk to Monmouth offers two options, a short cut taking a more direct route to the riverside at Symonds Yat or the full Wye Valley Walk route.

Option One - short cut to Symonds Yat East

Take the waymarked path at the northern end of the picnic area signed to Symonds Yat East and stick to the waymarked route, resisting all other paths however inviting they may appear. The path descends steeply, aided by steps and handrails, soon to reach and cross a metalled track. Continue down the hillside with the white houses of Symonds Yat West seen through the trees to reach the road and river by the Forest View and Royal hotels. (Note that the Saracen's Head Inn and ferry lie about 150 yards upstream to your right.) Take the path signed Monmouth 5³/₄ miles which is found on the left and passes the Royal Hotel car park.

Option Two - the full Wye Valley Walk route

From the Yat Rock viewpoint return to the road and take it northwards for 300 yards to take the path on the right signed to Welsh Bicknor. A steep descent is made down the hillside. Lichen-covered rocks, trailing vines

144

*Wye Valley Walk - the riverside between
Redbrook and Whitebrook*

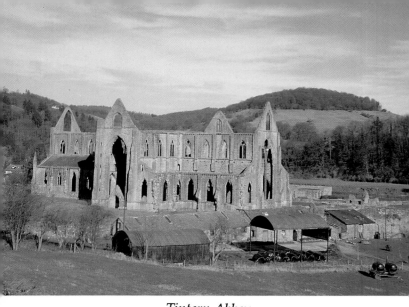

Tintern Abbey
Chepstow Castle

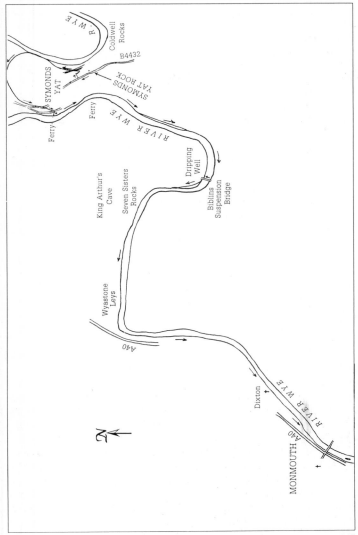

and the dense green combine to induce a jungle-like atmosphere, which is heightened on days when the mist still hangs over the river and clothes the forest in a diaphanous veil of mystery.

In a quarter of a mile the parting of the ways is signed. Ignore the invitation to Welsh Bicknor and turn left descending a rocky flight of steps to meet and cross a wide track. Continue down to reach the river bank and turn left. In season Himalayan Balsam, lines the banks, adding to the tropical flavour. In autumn you may reap a small harvest from an unexpected encounter with sweet chestnut trees - the trees were introduced to the Forest of Dean by the Romans and in later replanting of the forest one in every ten trees was a sweet chestnut.

The ruins of cottages being slowly choked by the luxuriant woodland growth are passed, nature reclaiming its own from the hand of man. A white cottage is seen on the left and after passing a couple of large rocks watch for the Wye Valley Walk waymark directing you to the left on a steeply rising path. This also coincides with a sign WVOF - footpath directions to Wye Valley Open Farm just beyond Huntsham Hill.

At the top of a short flight of steps turn right onto a forest road, and then almost immediately left to follow a path which soon makes a junction with a narrow road. Here turn left and follow the road for about 100 yards and take the path on the right which falls through the woods.

A further road is reached; cross this and go forward to the river and the ferry operated by the fifteenth-century inn on the opposite bank. Appropriately called the Ferrie Inn, its handsome reflection in the water demands the photographer's attention.

Do not cross the river. Follow the riverside path downstream with trees growing high upon the slopes above, amongst which a scatter of houses maintains a seemingly precarious but enviable foothold. A few minutes walking will bring you to the Saracen's Head Inn at Symonds Yat East where a further ferry crossing is in operation. Our route does not take us across the river yet but it is worth noting that the hand-operated ferry runs every 20 minutes during daylight hours (but not when the river is in flood).

Continue downstream to pass the Forest View and Royal hotels. Here take the path signed Monmouth 5¾ miles, which runs alongside the hotel car park. Soon the sound of the rapids will be heard ahead as you approach the islet in the river. Here canoeists practise their delicate art in their frail craft, a carefully balanced contest between the forces of nature and a nicely judged challenge.

The way follows the deep gorge of the Wye, with the cliffs rising sharply on both sides, the activities of the canoeists matched by climbers on the sheer rock faces - another carefully balanced contest.

As the track is joined by another coming in from the left, go forward on the lower and narrower of the paths, continuing under the trees. On the opposite bank an old mine level driven into the rocks may be seen close to a dripping well.

The map names the eastern side of the bank at this point as "The Slaughter". Traditionally it has been claimed as the site of a battle but no concrete evidence seems to be forthcoming to support the various stories which connect it with Caractacus and the Romans - about which many tales abound - or clashes in later ages which involved the Danes, the Vikings or a little local difficulty during the Civil War.

About 1¾ miles downstream from Symonds Yat East the crossing of the river is made by way of the Biblins suspension bridge erected by the Forestry Commission, a mild adventure totally in keeping with the jungle-like atmosphere stirred up by the imagination on the descent from Yat Rock.

Once safely over the bridge, turn left, signposted Monmouth 4¼ miles and follow the riverside once again. As you progress the towering white limestone bluffs of the Seven Sisters come into view. Our way lies beneath the cliffs but from these unfenced edges there is a fine and unfettered prospect of the Wye. A few minutes' walking from the Seven Sisters is King Arthur's cave, its connection with the heroic figure somewhat tenuous, but it should be remembered that we are now only a few short miles from the birthplace of Geoffrey of Monmouth. It was this twelfth-century monk who retold the stories of Arthur in his *History of the Kings of Britain - Historia Regum Brittanniae*. From this has descended many an heroic epic of varying degrees of merit. More concretely the interest in the cave lies in its occupation by prehistoric man and the discovery during excavations of the bones of such fearsome creatures as lions, woolly rhinoceros, cave bears and mammoths.

A quarter of a mile from the bridge the path enters the woods, walking a little above what is a delightful stretch of the river. Soon the way is passing under the Seven Sisters; to your right the rock cliffs rise sheer through the trees disappearing through the canopy to the lofty viewpoints.

As the woods are left behind the A40 can be seen ahead cutting across

High above the Wye on the Seven Sisters

a hillside, perhaps with a buzzard to be seen circling the sky over the woods.
Cross the meadow where white cattle graze, clearly well used to walkers for
they totally ignore them. To the right can be seen the turreted towers of the
house at Wyastone Leys with its commanding view down the Wye.

148

Quiet and hopeful fishermen in boats moored in the river contrast with the increasing roar of the A40 as the path turns to run parallel, but underneath it. Here the river makes a further sharp turn then keeps what passes for it as an unaccustomed and virtuously straight, well, straightish course, for the next two miles to Monmouth.

From the bend hug the riverside on a pleasant shaded path at first with the river sparkling away a few feet below. The wooded section gives way to open fields about the point where the "Welcome to Wales" sign is seen away to the right on the A40 together in spring with the welcoming drifts of daffodils. Out of sight of the motorists and truck drivers, a great bank of primroses offers its own greeting to the walkers keeping company with the free living, free flowing, sparkling Wye.

Go on over the meadows to cross a stream by a bridge and swing left to continue downstream as the outskirts of Monmouth come into view. The little turreted, stumpy-spired church of Saint Peter's, Dixton, is met, and the way lies through the churchyard through a small iron gate mysteriously carrying the initials NCE. The church has been stoutly padlocked on occasions when I have passed it. By each door is a small stack of sandbags bearing testimony to the floodings it suffers in its low-lying position.

Soon the spire of another and larger church rises skywards - Saint Mary's, Monmouth. Another stage in the long journey down the Wye is nearly complete, but still a fair step to the sea with the tidal waters yet to be met.

The path continues through a succession of fields, kissing gates and over little streams adding their widow's mite to the river. Then the Wye bridge comes into sight and the great hill to your left with the wireless masts is the Kymin where yet more of our long history is remembered but for the moment Monmouth awaits.

Leave the river by the bridge and cross the busy A40 by the subway to explore Monmouth and raise your cap in salute to one of our most celebrated warrior kings and a hero of more modern, but sadly no less warlike, times.

25: Monmouth

Most towns are known by a key picture that identifies them. Monmouth has one, the Monnow Bridge Gate, a tall, slender fortress built around 1260 as part of the town's defences. It was not uncommon in its day but is now the only surviving example in Britain of a fortified bridge gateway of a medieval walled town.

Monmouth's strategic importance at the meeting of two rivers at one of the gateways to Wales was not lost on the Romans. Their station, Blestium, was later used as the site for the castle built by William Fitz-Osbern shortly after the Norman Conquest. As so often happened the security offered by the castle encouraged the growth of the town which expanded around its walls. In the mid-thirteenth century the lordship and castle were granted to the eldest son of Henry III, who in 1272 succeeded to the throne as Edward I. Edward passed the title and castle on to his younger brother, Edmund, Earl of Lancaster. It was a troublesome time throughout the kingdom and in 1277 Edmund was engaged in the war against the man who had been earlier recognised by Henry as the Prince of Wales, Llywelyn ap Gruffudd.

It was in 1387 that the lusty cry of a new born child rang round the stone walls of the castle. The cry was to be echoed 27 years later as Monmouth's most famous son, Henry V, leading a tired and seemingly hopelessly outnumbered army, defeated the French at Agincourt.

The castle was slighted in 1647, following the dark days of the Civil War and only a small portion of it remains today. The Marquess of Worcester built his Great Castle House nearby in 1673, the location determined by his wish that the forthcoming birth of a grandson should be close to the birthplace of the hero of Agincourt. The Castle House is now the headquarters of the Royal Monmouthshire Engineers. The gun that stands on the forecourt was captured from the Russians at Sebastopol in 1856.

Henry is more publicly remembered by a rather pale statue on the front of the Shire Hall built in 1724. I must confess that I much prefer the more stylised representation on the inn sign which bears his name. Here he is seen as a warrior king, armed with a lance and in a headlong ferocious charge that would have surely ensured victory in any battle. It was at the Shire Hall in 1840 that members of the Chartist movement, among them John Frost, a former Mayor of Newport, faced charges of treason. The trial followed the violent but abortive uprising in Newport the previous November when over twenty supporters of the movement were killed. The advantage of hindsight suggests that the petitions contained in the People's Charter were by no means unreasonable. Indeed they listed many things which we take for granted today. Demands were made for the vote for all members of the adult male population, election by ballot, salaries for Members of Parliament and equal electoral constituencies. Frost and his associates were found guilty and condemned to death, a sentence that, wisely, was not carried out, and they were transported to Australia. Further petitions presented to Parliament were rejected and the movement lost impetus, defeated perhaps by the resort to arms, but nevertheless a slow fuse had been lit which in time led to the reforms that the Chartists were seeking.

In front of the Shire Hall is the very likable statue commemorating the many achievements of the Hon Charles Stewart Rolls, as the inscription records: "a pioneer in both scientific and practical motoring and aviation". He was the first man to fly from England to France and back without landing. His life was cut short at the early age of thirty-three when his plane crashed at Bournemouth in 1910. By that time his association with Royce had ensured that he will be remembered whenever their names are joined together as symbols of fine engineering.

Rolls is depicted holding a model biplane in his hand but it was the great cavalcade of the famous cars that processed through the town to mark the centenary of his birth that he might most have appreciated as a tribute to his memory. What a sight that must have been!

Excavations during 1990 "looking for the town wall" revealed a quantity of silt and sand deposited on the site of a fourteenth-century house in Monnow Street during a great flood. Troubles never come singly for it seems that the flooding may have coincided with the Black Death of 1348. Other finds included a medieval silver

The Hon. Chas Rolls remembered in Agincourt Square, Monmouth

penny, iron slag from forges of the thirteenth and fourteenth centuries, and two butchers' pole-axes suggesting the existence of a slaughter house on the site.

Monmouth was one of a series of ports along the river engaged in the forging of iron and the export of oak bark - for tanning - and perhaps the most famous industry, the manufacture of Monmouth Caps of which Shakespeare makes mention in Henry V. A priory of the Benedictine order was established in the town after the Norman Conquest and has been associated with the scribe, Geoffrey of Monmouth, to whom we owe the *History of the Kings of Britain* from which the great Arthurian legends are descended.

Nelson stayed in Monmouth during a visit to the Forest of Dean to inspect timber required for the navy. A collection of Nelson memorabilia together with items of local history can be seen at the museum in Priory Street. An impressive feature of today's town is the extensive grammar school founded by William Jones in 1614 and rebuilt and extended in 1865 by the Worshipful Company of the Haberdashers of London. A piece of more modern history is reflected in the wrought iron gates which were installed in 1961 having been salvaged from the Haberdashers' Hall following the German bombing of London in 1941.

When you stand on Monnow Bridge to compose your souvenir photograph of the fortified gateway your attention may be drawn to the white tower high on Kymin Hill. This is the Round House, a dining club built by the gentlemen of Monmouth. Close by is the Naval Temple which was "erected Aug 1 1800, to perpetuate the names of those noble admirals who distinguished themselves by glorious victories for England in the last and present wars...".

No fewer than sixteen victories between 1759 and 1801 are commemorated by individual plaques bearing the names of admirals, famous names like Hawke, Hood, How, Cornwallis, Rodney, Vincent and, of course, Nelson. The temple is crowned by a triumphant Britannia seated on a rock - you can almost hear the distant strains of Thomas Arne's Rule Britannia, although it predates the earliest of the events celebrated, having been first performed in 1740, in the amphitheatre close to the Thames at Clliveden. By a strange coincidence the first public hearing was on August 1, the same month and day shown on the plaque recording the opening of the temple.

The temple and tower lie on the route of the Offa's Dyke Path National Trail and a diversion via this can be taken with a return to the Wye Valley Walk at Redbrook.

The unique fortified gatehouse on Monnow Bridge, Monmouth

26: Monmouth to Tintern

DISTANCE:	11$^{1}/_{2}$ miles approx.
DETAIL:	5 miles pleasant riverside and wooded walking then ascent to follow a forested ridge for 4$^{1}/_{2}$ miles with fine views. Descending to Brockweir Bridge with level walking to complete the section at Tintern Abbey.
DIVERSION TO KYMIN HILL:	See opening text - will increase distance by 1 mile approx.
MAPS:	Outdoor Leisure Map No.14 - The Wye Valley (1:25,000) or Landranger Sheet 162 - (1:50,000).
ACCOMMODATION:	Monmouth. Llandogo. Brockweir. Tintern.
TRAVEL:	Red and White bus operates between Monmouth and Chepstow.
TOILETS:	Monmouth. Whitestone picnic site (FC) Tintern.
SHOPS:	Monmouth, Redbrook, Tintern.
TOURIST INFORMATION:	Church Street, Monmouth, Gwent. NP5 3BX (0600 3899) Tintern Abbey, Gwent. NP6 6TE (0291 689431)

Motorists travelling in the early spring to Monmouth by the A40 are greeted as they cross the boundary into Gwent by great banks of daffodils - an inspired and heart lifting "say it with flowers" welcome to Wales. It also helps set the scene for this section of the walk which is particularly rewarding after the dead days of winter with a wealth of wild flowers to brighten the way.

Kymin Hill is a very visible feature of the Monmouth landscape rising to 820 feet with fine views of the Wye Valley and the hill country around this former county town. With so many viewpoints along the route it may be tempting to give this one a miss but an added incentive is the Naval Temple erected in 1800 to honour the victories of a pride of British admirals over a forty-year period. If this is likely to be your only opportunity to pay your respects to Nelson and his colleagues then you may like to abandon the first couple of miles of the Wye Valley Walk from Monmouth and rejoin it at Redbrook.

Diversion to take in Kymin Naval Temple

From Monmouth cross the Wye Bridge by the A466 Redbrook Road and ignore the path signed Wye Valley Walk. Keep with the road until it bears to the right. At this point go forward to follow the A4136 for about 250 yards to take a path on the right signed Kymin 1 mile, Sedbury Cliffs 17 miles. From here on keep with the Offa's Dyke Path waymarking into Upper Redbrook as follows: Take the rising path through trees which is left by a kissing gate to follow a track for a short distance to join a narrow lane. Go forward and in about 300 yards enter Garth Wood. Take the rising waymarked path which leads to a field after a few minutes' walking. Take the field path, roughly southwards, for 300 yards to reach a lane after crossing a stile. Turn left and in a few yards take the path on the left and climb through the wood to reach the summit of Kymin Hill. (Details of the Naval Temple are contained in Monmouth notes.)

Continue southward from the temple on a path with a garden on your left and a wood on your right to emerge into an open field. Maintain your direction over fields for about 700 yards and when a large barn (shortly to be converted into a house) is seen on your right, cross the stile on your right to join Duffields Lane. Turn left with this and follow it over open hillside, losing height as Duffield Farm is passed on your left. Swing right with the track about 300 yards after passing the farm and continue to join the Lydbrook-Redbrook road. Keep with the road for about 600 yards, leaving the Offa's Dyke Path to go its own way when it filters off left. On reaching the A466 by the Bush Inn rejoin the Wye Valley Way as described from Redbrook.

Wye Valley Route

Cross the Wye by the many-arched stone bridge and take the path on the right signed to Redbrook, soon to follow the edge of a fine sports ground with a multiplicity of rugby pitches, confirmation that we are indeed in Wales. At the end of the sports ground cross under the bridge that once

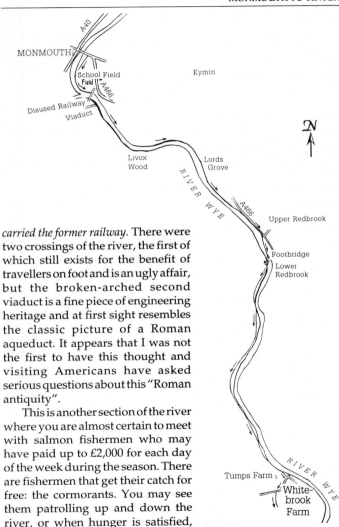

carried the former railway. There were two crossings of the river, the first of which still exists for the benefit of travellers on foot and is an ugly affair, but the broken-arched second viaduct is a fine piece of engineering heritage and at first sight resembles the classic picture of a Roman aqueduct. It appears that I was not the first to have this thought and visiting Americans have asked serious questions about this "Roman antiquity".

This is another section of the river where you are almost certain to meet with salmon fishermen who may have paid up to £2,000 for each day of the week during the season. There are fishermen that get their catch for free: the cormorants. You may see them patrolling up and down the river, or when hunger is satisfied, gathered together on a favourite tree

157

The wide ranging view from Kymin.
Monmouth in the foreground, The Sugar Loaf in the far distance - centre.

to dry out their feathers.

Here between the two bridges the river tumbles singing over yet another rapid with the birds along the wooded edges providing a descant. In spring the paths are lined with celandine, and later as we pass through the riverside edge of Lords Grove, violets, primroses and wood anemones combine to provide a wild bouquet.

After the wooded section the path emerges into the meadows, the way punctuated by a series of stiles. On the river's edge mussel shells lie empty, the inner sides shining like mother of pearl, each a jewel in its own right.

To the right Livox Wood rises steeply and beyond it riverside pastures where swans as well as sheep graze. It seems to be a popular spot with often a score or more to be seen in the fields. On the left Kymin Hill rises to over 800 feet and then the long bank of Lords Grove, the trees arrayed in many shades of green.

The path edges close to the road, but whilst the traffic may be heard it is unseen until the walker is obliged to join it a little short of Redbrook. Once out of the woods again the path follows a narrow strip of pasture and several large rocks are seen in the river - a hazard to navigation. Even highly *manoeuvrable canoes in skilled hands must be in danger in waters such as this.*

Just beyond the rocks the path decants onto the road. Go forward to the Bush Inn at Redbrook.

Redbrook - there are two centres, Upper and Lower - was once associated with the iron industry that was established early in the seventeenth century. Fast-flowing streams supplied power and in the eighteenth century copper was smelted in the area, with a tin plate industry developing that survived until the early 1960s.

Take the path opposite the Bush Inn that runs between the road and river and in 300 yards climb steps. Turn left and go forward for a few yards to fish hook back right to the footbridge which crosses the river parallel with the former railway bridge. At this point the walker has briefly crossed the border of Wales from Gwent into Gloucestershire and about midway over the bridge back into Wales again.

Across the river is the Boat Inn with refreshments, real ale and the pungent smell of wood smoke and three (or is it four?) waterfalls tumbling down the rocks at its back door. On reaching the lane, turn sharp right and pass under the bridge to follow the river downstream for about half a mile.

Just after passing the first of the green fishing huts, take the path signed off right to join the old railway track. Turn left with the track and follow it for a mile and a half to reach Tumps Farm at the foot of the Whitebrook Valley. That brightly coloured bird, the jay, may be seen or heard in the area. Its harsh cry is a direct contrast to its attractive plumage and likely to attract your attention to its presence before you catch sight of the bird. The jay is an acorn eater and like the squirrel provides itself with a harvest store, burying the acorns for use in winter. A little cannibalism does not come amiss for it will plunder the nests of other birds for eggs and fledglings.

The track runs well above the river out of danger of winter floods. Here the Wye is wide and almost free flowing, almost because, in common with other stretches of the river, weirs hold back the water, providing deeper pools to aid the fishing.

Turn right up the lane, passing Tump Farm and in 300 yards, just after passing Whitebrook Farm, take the steeply rising path on the left. At the top of the first rise pause to view the valley. What a change from the days when this was another of the industrial valleys along the Wye, a black and white industry, black for its wire works which were

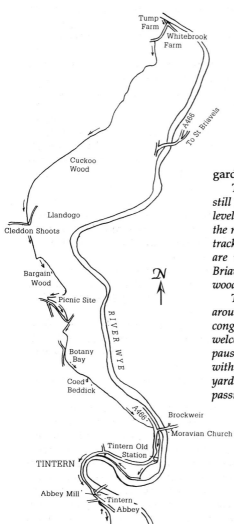

succeeded by paper mills with products which included the high quality paper required for bank notes! Now in spring the valley is a special delight, the relics of industry now mature ruins, or the three-storied mills converted to houses, a totally peaceful retreat, bright with pink and white blossom in its gardens.

Turn left from this viewpoint, still gaining height for the high level part of this section. At top of the next pitch swing left onto the track. As the path levels out there are views over the river to St Briavels and bluebells mass in the woods.

The lane is followed to the green around which a scatter of houses congregates and a seat offers a welcome break, a suitable point to pause for refreshment. Continue with the lane for a further 100 yards then turn left (just after passing the gateway to Spring Cottage). Keep with the wide track with most of the uphill work now finished. When the path divides, take the right fork which rises to join a metalled lane.

Turn left and follow the lane for about 700 yards to enter Cuckoo Wood just after passing Moor Cottage. A broad path takes you through the wood with breaks in the trees offering views down to the river and the houses set on the opposite hillside, and downstream the tall towers of the Severn Bridge.

The hilltop village of St Briavels across the valley, was once heavily engaged in the manufacture of cross-bow bolts. The Norman castle was the administrative centre for the Forest of Dean but now does duty as a youth hostel. Previous guests include King John who stopped here on hunting trips to the forest. Join the YHA and stop in all the best places, for they do indeed have a wide variety of hostels in both splendid buildings and locations! I met a small group of American teenagers backpacking their way up the Wye Valley and they enquired how far to St Briavels? What a tale to tell when they got back home - sleeping in an English castle where King John had regularly stayed.

About half a mile after entering Cuckoo Wood the broad forest road is left at a point where it swings past the remains of a shed. A waymarked post should be present to direct you forward to follow a narrower but clear path. The path falls gently to meet a narrow road at Cleddon about ³/₄ of a mile above Llandogo.

Here accommodation seekers, or those with a bus to catch should head downhill, but not before stopping to enjoy the falling waters of Cleddon Shoots, a pleasing series of cataracts that tumble down the hillside, falling over 500 feet in the course of half a mile.

From Cleddon Shoots take the path signed Tintern which in a short distance divides into three. Take the middle way which leads to Bargain Wood. In about 300 yards turn left to a series of viewpoints with seats provided for the comfortable enjoyment of the prospect.

The wide track runs steadily downhill to the Forestry Commission's Whitestone Picnic Site, with adventure playground and toilets. Pass through the barrier and go forward half-right along a forest road. As the motor road is approached, take the path on the left through pines and follow this for about a quarter of a mile to meet road by Jubilee Plantation. This was planted by the National Committee for Wales in 1979. At the road bear left with it for a few yards then take path on the right signed to Tintern. The path falls through trees to cross a stream with the aid of stepping stones. A further stream is crossed and a patch of open ground is seen to the left with the path following the inside edge of the wood along the line of an old wall.

A lane is reached; here turn left, passing the entrance to the Gwent CC

Scout Council Camping Activity Centre at Botany Bay.

After passing a white house on your left, turn left to enter the forest again, Coed Beddick. The path opens out to a broad, rising track, eventually with views down the steep slopes to the river. On reaching an old wall, go forward for a few yards then left, steeply downhill, with views across the river to the neat gardens of Brockweir. The path soon swings to the right and descends to meet the road near Brockweir bridge. (Caution - overhanging branches may obscure approaching traffic.)

Turn right and cross to the bridge; before continuing pause to take a look at Brockweir lying across the river. A more peaceful place can scarcely be imagined - a tiny riverside village with its bankside houses reflected in the waters of the Wye, a quiet country pub, the inevitable village store, the lifeline of small communities, a little white-painted chapel, and green pastures beyond rising to meet the wooded hilltops.

It was not always thus. Turn back the clock as we have so often done on our journey down the Wye. The atmosphere of quiet inactivity has vanished. Instead of the fly fisherman hopefully making yet another cast over the rippling waters there is a great bustle. Waggons trundle down the hillside bringing timber for the shipbuilding industry, and other waggons haul goods to or from the quayside, for this was also a riverside port. It was a point of interchange with cargoes from larger ships which had negotiated the tidal waters to their limit being transferred to shallow draught barges to be hauled further upstream by men and horses. A picture of riverside commerce - men earning their living by hard work, boat builders, dockers, traders, ships' chandlers, and sailors. So far, so good. The day's work is done - does peace gradually replace the clamour of the work place as twilight falls and men return to their homes? Not so. This little settlement, too small to have a church, yet could muster no less than seven cider houses in the 1830s! Wages hard earned, and indeed they were, went all too easily to quench thirsts and over indulgence led to disputes and fighting. Pretty little Brockweir as we see it today had an unenviable reputation as a lawless, godless place.

It was this sad state of affairs that led to the building of the Moravian church. A doctor from nearby Tintern was greatly concerned at the unrestrained disorder and appealed to the Moravian church in Bristol for help in 1831. The Moravians had a missionary zeal, and brave men that they were, armed with the courage of their convictions, accepted the challenge. The minister who had been given responsibility for bringing Christianity to Brockweir set sail from Bristol to lay the foundation stone in 1832 and on May 7, 1833, the church was opened.

From the western side of the bridge descend the steps and go forward for a quarter of a mile to reach Tintern Old Station. Along the way you will note a succession of bat boxes secured to the trees. Unlike the more usual nest boxes, they do not have a hole at the front but a narrow gap at the bottom.

Tintern Station has been restored to a neat Victorian country railway station with notices announcing a Great Western Railway excursion to a military exhibition at Chelsea Royal Hospital in 1890. There is car parking and a picnic site, with the station and exhibition with refreshments open from Easter. Coaches in the livery of the Great Western Railway are to be seen on a short length of track, but the only train that operates is a tiny model railway, greatly dwarfed by the signal box.

Follow the track bed from the signal box until the river is reached. The bridge has been dismantled, but as you descend on the right to the river bank it is clear what a fine view passengers must have had of the Wye and the hills. Follow the river bank until Saint Michael's Church is reached. The path runs through its churchyard, beyond which you turn left behind houses, soon to reach the road, and go forward to Tintern. The church, despite a long history of flooding, was built on low-lying land, and with an expected high tide the churchwarden was removing the carpets from the floor in anticipation of water once again pouring into the building.

When the tide is in at Tintern the water is close to the top of the bank, and sandbags are stacked by doors of shops, houses and pubs with good cause.

It is around the time of the March high tides that some strange activity may be noticed. As evening arrives long poles with stout muslin nets and buckets are seen along the banks for a considerable distance, unattended until dusk arrives when men with strong torches take up position on the river bank. The uninitiated arriving along this stretch of the river after dark might be deceived into thinking that giant-sized glow worms had unaccountably developed or that stories of will-o'-the-wisps had some basis of truth. The reality that is being witnessed is the annual run of elvers which takes place for about three weeks around the spring tides. Countless millions of elvers, carried by the ocean currents from the Sargasso Sea into our waters, migrate upstream. Only three inches long, they swim into the network of rivers and canals to grow to adulthood, before, like their parents, making the long journey back to the Atlantic spawning grounds of the Sargasso - another of nature's great mysteries. These immature eels are prized as a great delicacy by some and there is an export trade to Spain. They are also used for the stocking of continental rivers. The large number of nets, bright lights and buckets are testimony to the value of the catch, which, it is said, can fetch as much as £50 a pound!

Just past the Moon and Sixpence look downstream to the ruins of the old chapel high on the hill above Tintern. On then into the village, busy in summer with its tourist trade, antique shops and ample accommodation.

Just by the abbey a handsomely decorated Romany caravan of 1894 was on view for some time awaiting a buyer, a Ledge Romani Wagon, built by Day and Fairbrother of Royton, Lancashire, the only remaining wagon constructed by the firm. It is said once to have belonged to Natin Lock (née Wood), a famous family of Welsh gypsies who were the last to use the pure form of the Romany language.

And so to the ruins of the great abbey that created so much interest for the writers, poets and artists making the Wye Tour.

27: Tintern

It is interesting to reflect that the abbey has stood longer in its roofless, ruined state then as a place of worship, a tribute to its builders if not to those who stripped the protecting lead from its roof and filched its stone.

Walter FitzRichard, Lord of Chepstow, is the acknowledged founder of the abbey. In 1131 he invited monks from the Cistercian Order in France to settle here in the quiet of this tidal river valley. The order was dedicated to the precepts laid down by a Dorset man, the saintly Stephen Harding, who, having studied at Sherborne, entered the monastic life in France becoming abbot at Citeaux. In essence he preached a gospel of the simple lifestyle, a disdain of worldly riches and comforts which he believed served only to distract his monks from their vocation.

The foundation flourished under the patronage of the nobility with grants of land adding to the income. Extensions in 1220 lead to rebuilding in 1270 by Roger Bigod III, with the new church an impressive building of cathedral-like dimensions. Clustered around the church were the domestic buildings, kitchens, dining hall, dormitories for monks and lay brothers, accommodation for novices, an infirmary to care for the sick, cloisters, a library and so on.

Tintern Abbey is best appreciated on a quiet day when the imagination may be allowed to work its magic, fleshing out the skeleton of the buildings, restoring the low walls that are all that remain of its ancillary buildings, filling them with the monks and lay brothers who worked and worshipped here over a period of 400 years.

Standing at the western end of the church looking down the nave and into the chancel presents a picture of a fine building - remarkable that it still remains here some 450 years after the Dissolution was set to destroy it. In the quietness there is a strong feeling that this is still a holy place. High arched windows, in places the delicate tracery still intact, reach up to the sky in silent stone prayer. The eye is led on to the distant wooded heights framed by the glassless east window. It is tempting mentally to join the monks in the words of the Psalm as they too must have "lifted their eyes unto the hills". But it is only the birds that remain today to offer evensong.

It could not have been an easy life despite the endowments and patronage of the rich and powerful. The lay brothers would have had a hard regime of work on the farms that helped support the abbey. However rewarding to the spirit the contemplative life might have been, the discipline of attending seven daily services starting as early as two in the morning removes any suggestion that the religious life was a comfortable retreat from the rigours of the outside world.

The chill wind that blows through the ruins on a March day leaves one in no doubt that this was no easy life and the presence of a warming house reinforces the discomforts that had to be endured. High on the wooded ridge above the abbey a stone column has acquired the status of The Devil's Pulpit. Here he is supposed to have called upon the monks to renounce their faith. Could it be that the Devil, attempting to seduce the monks away from their devotions, was not offering the erotic pleasures of the flesh that might be imagined but the simple comforts of a full night's sleep in a warm bed?

The picture of grey cowled monks haunting the stairs and alleys which the early Wye tourists came to romanticise cannot be left to stand unchallenged as the only image, however dramatic its appeal. There was much work to be done: the sick and aged to be cared for in the infirmary, the novices to be instructed, perhaps the sons of rich patrons to be educated, and the abbey's estates required skilled management if they were to give a proper return.

"Give us this day our daily bread," prayed the monks as we still do today. In furtherance of the appeal to God the lay brothers went forth to the farms, the forest and the fisheries to fulfil this basic need. Tintern was not for ever a remote place of peace cut off from the world as the founding members first knew it and it was not only in the field that the brothers laboured. Some were engaged in the production of iron, an industry introduced to the area by the Cistercians. In 1568, only thirty years after the monks had departed, brass was first made by alloying copper with zinc. The forges created by the monks continued as an expanding local industry, aided by the plentiful supply of timber for charcoal, with wire making a speciality. Iron ore had been mined in the Forest of Dean for a thousand years before the Romans came to exploit its mineral wealth.

The pilgrims of one age are the tourists of the next and sightseers have been making their way to Tintern for more than 200 years. The lower Wye valley and Tintern in particular had a strong attraction for writers, poets, painters and engravers as the print room at the Chepstow Museum amply demonstrates. The diarist, Viscount Torrington (John Byng) had his own ideas how the abbey should best be enjoyed. He recommended a picnic within the ruins with cold meats and wines with a Welsh harper brought from Chepstow to provide a suitable musical accompaniment.

These early visitors came by boat, rowed downstream from Ross-on-Wye, with stops to enjoy the famed views from Yat Rock, the mysticism of Tintern and the great stone fortress of Chepstow Castle. Less frivolously, sailing boats rode up on the tide to provide a two-way trade to the ports of the lower Wye. The coming of the railway brought many more visitors with a 13-mile scenic route between Chepstow and Monmouth. It was built in 1874 with the commercial traffic of the area in mind, tunnels being cut through the rock at Tiddenham and Tintern. Intermediate stations were built at Tiddenham, Tintern, Brockweir and Redbrook. The line continued to serve industry and the community until 1959. The old station at Tintern has been given a new lease of life as the starting point of waymarked walks, with a picnic site and a railway exhibition telling the story of the line.

The smoke of the iron furnaces has drifted away, rail and sail have departed, and only the abbey stones remain as a monument to the work and worship of the past.

Note: The remains of one of Tintern's foundries can be visited on the Forestry Commission's waymarked Tintern Trail. A leaflet *Walks in Tintern Woods* describes this and other walks and is available at Tourist Information Centres in the area.

28: Tintern to Chepstow

DISTANCE:	5 miles approx.
DETAIL:	A strenuous climb to a wooded ridge, to pursue the forest above Black Cliff until at the Wyndcliff the Eagles Nest reveals all. Descent by the 365 steps to Lower Wyndcliff with further woodland walking to reach Chepstow.
MAPS:	Outdoor Leisure Map No.14. The Wye Valley (1:25,000) or Landranger Sheet 162 (1:50,000).
ACCOMMODATION:	Tintern. Chepstow.
TOILETS:	Tintern. Chepstow.
SHOPS:	Tintern. Chepstow.
TOURIST INFORMATION:	Tintern Abbey. (0291 689431) The Gate House, High Street, Chepstow, Gwent. NP6 5LH (02912 3772)

From the Royal George, Tintern, go forward to take the lane that runs behind Abbey Antiques. In a short distance a waymark on a telegraph pole will confirm that you are on the right track. Soon the abbey comes into view and behind it the steep wooded slopes across the Wye with the rock column known as the Devil's Pulpit leaning out from the cliff edge and hidden in the trees. It was from here that the Devil, who must have been gifted with an exceptionally loud voice, is popularly supposed to have preached to the monks and lay brothers of the abbey, offering the usual earthy inducements to forsake more heavenly pursuits.

Beyond the houses the metalled lane becomes a track; ignore the sign to Black Cliff and continue forward rising steadily up the valley between twin hillsides. The track deepens into a hollow way and is perfumed, if that rather delicate word can be used in these circumstances, by the pungent smelling ramson. When the plants burst forth into bloom in April and May the purity suggested by their visually attractive white star-shaped flowers is greatly diminished by the overpowering smell of garlic

168

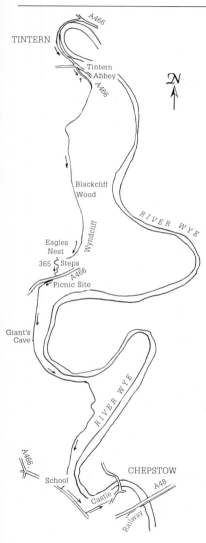

hanging heavily on the air.

This is yet another sheltered habitat for birds and their spring chorus is performed as loudly and enthusiastically here as anywhere along the route.

Just under half a mile from entering the wood, a little beyond a rocky outcrop, bear left to cross the stream that has accompanied you up the hillside, and fish hook left on a narrow rising path. After levelling out the path bears right up a stepped bank then forward to meet a stile and emerge into an open field.

Cross the field in line with the post which carries a waymark and as the wood opposite is reached, swing a little to the left for 60 yards to cross a stile into a wood. Take the rising path half-right and in about 250 yards swing to the left with it, then soon right and then again left to reach the ridge top of Black Cliff Wood. The passage along the 750-foot ridge is almost viewless with only the odd glimpse of the river below and none at all when the mist hangs over the valley.

When a metal gate is seen to your right with wireless masts to the west, the path does a little wiggle, but the generally southward direction is maintained. The inside edge of the wood is followed

169

for a short distance as the way swings to the south-west to reach the Eagles Nest viewpoint 700 feet above the river on the Wyndcliff.

Here is the reward for the seemingly long imprisonment of the trees, shut off from the outside world. A high window in the forest has been thrown open to reveal the green woods below, the great loop of the Wye where its snake-like writhing seems just to fail to link up with itself. Strangely it is the Wye itself that we have so faithfully followed these long miles that takes something away from a fine and atmospheric prospect. Here the flow is strongly tidal, with a rise and fall at Chepstow of 49 feet, an alternating two-way movement that is responsible for a change in its generally cheerful character. The river does not take on the pastel shades of its wooded surrounds, nor yet in chameleon fashion reflecting the greys and blues of the sky above. The ebb and flow have induced an uncharacteristic fit of depression; fearful perhaps of the future as it loses its separate identity, it has donned a dowdy dress of muddy brown. Only looking directly towards the sunlight does it manage a little of its normal sparkling form.

Beyond the Wye cliffs of Wintours Leap flows the Severn, over a mile wide with great sandbanks clogging this mighty artery. Downstream the topmost ramparts of Chepstow Castle high above the Wye are dwarfed by the more distant 400-feet-high towers of the Severn Bridge, with the grey pylons of the national grid beyond. And onwards the great expanse of the Severn Estuary merges into the grey-blue haze of a world beyond our ken.

The walker pausing to take in the view may take his rest upon a seat which commemorates the work of Chris Pugh, a Wye Valley warden from 1972 to 1983. The thought must cross the minds of many who pass this way that this is a fine place to be remembered. Will our own virtues be marked in similar fashion one day?

From the Eagles Nest climb the steps and bear left. After a short distance a sign points the way, (left) to the 365 steps. Here is a relic of the romance of the Wye tours of the eighteenth and nineteenth centuries. The steps, presumably deliberately mirroring the number of the days of the year, were installed in 1828 to carry the pilgrims of the day to the top of the limestone cliff. The way was eased but with sufficient effort required to encourage them in the belief that they had earned the reward of the twin views of Wye and Severn.

Walking through the Giant's Cave on route to Chepstow

Make the twisting descent to the road aided by the steps and the occasional handrail, perhaps counting as you go. Two things are certain, that no two people are likely to arrive at an agreed total and whatever the tally it will be some weeks short of a full calendar. Time has once again taken its accustomed toll.

171

From the quarry at the foot of the steps cross the road to the Forestry Commission's Lower Wyndcliff picnic site. Here the birds find rich pickings, chaffinches and robins needing little bidding to join walkers at their meal with the more cautious black-capped great tits only just out of arm's reach.

From the car park take the south-west path at first close to the road but soon edging away into the forest: a rising and falling path, stepped here and there, with the land falling away sharply to the Wye far below. In a little over half a mile from the car park the terraced path plunges into the Giant's Cave and out again. Maintain direction over Piercefield Cliffs. Chepstow Racecourse is above your head and out of sight. A further cave with a narrow entrance is passed on your right as the walk continues along the edge of the rock face. Below are the Apostles Rocks, a series of bluffs above the river. As the Wye starts yet another of its loops the path veers away into Pierce Wood, ducking under a laurel archway to pass the remains of an igloo-like building - ice house, grotto or an old kiln?

The path falls through the woods, the way marked at frequent intervals by yellow blobs on the trunks. The path rises again to keep closer company with the Wye and to give a glimpse of Chepstow Castle through the branches. Suddenly, as with the Eagles Nest, the veil is fully lifted and the walker is favoured with a fine view downstream to the castle high on the cliffs above the river.

From the viewpoint climb the stepped path to reach an old stone wall and in a few yards turn left through a gap in the wall. The path edges the Chepstow Leisure Centre to decant into the car park, instant civilisation that comes rather too quickly with no gradual acclimatisation from country to town.

From the car park go forward to meet the road and turn left with it. Immediately the first impressions of Chepstow are good: a fine school and leisure centre combined, clean streets and pleasant architecture with the smell of the sea carried faintly on the breeze.

After a short walk turn left through the dell to complete the long trek down the Wye Valley beneath the great fortress of Chepstow Castle, an appropriate full stop to a memorable journey.

29: Chepstow

Chepstow is a marvellously atmospheric place at which to end or begin a journey such as ours. It is, of course, a border town, the Gateway to Wales: the bridge over the Wye an unguarded, uncustomed border suitably marked at its centre span in letters picked out in gold "Anno Domini 1816 Monmouth Gloucester". John Rennie, the noted Scottish engineer, having inspected a decaying earlier bridge, rejected the notion of effecting repairs and proposed an entirely new structure. His advice could hardly be ignored for his achievements included London's Waterloo Bridge, the design for London Bridge, which his son was to complete, and the Kennet and Avon Canal. Construction was in the hands of John Rastrick, another noted engineer who in 1808 had built the world's first passenger locomotive engine from Richard Trevithick's design.

Just a little downstream another famous engineer, the incomparable and grandly named Isambard Kingdom Brunel, was to put his talents to work with the railway bridge that opened in 1852. The designers and engineers responsible for the 1966 suspension bridge carrying the M4 motorway over both the Severn and Wye must have been very conscious that they were following in famous footsteps when they set about their task. The statistics are impressive: total length 5,240 feet, two 400-feet towers to suspend the 3,240-feet central span and traffic that would have astonished even the far-seeing eyes of Rennie, Rastrick and Brunel.

Chepstow and the Wye have long been an important centre with the town engaged in ship building using the plentiful supply of timber, the transportation of stone from the quarries of the region, and a considerable wine importing business. Farmers brought their goods to market here and a milling industry thrived. Today Stuart Crystal exports its high quality products world wide, with a visitor centre in the Old Board School, close to the castle, which offers regular tours of this fascinating craft. Even today the town's name is not far removed from its Saxon origin which quite literally means market place.

A walk along the river front amply demonstrates the huge tidal rise and fall, some 49 feet, with the scouring river flowing muddy brown through the town as it does for most of its tidal range, an unwelcome contrast with the clean, clear waters that we have enjoyed for most of our journey down the river. A plate set into the bridge indicates the high tide of the flood of October 17, 1883, which would have clearly made its way into the Bridge Inn.

Ship building took on a desperate urgency during the First World War with a dramatic revival of the industry that had flourished during previous centuries. Workers were drafted into Chepstow in 1917 from the traditional ship yard towns of Tyneside as thousands of Royal Engineers worked flat out to build new yards to facilitate the replacement of the disastrous losses of a long war of attrition.

Many of the voyages made from Chepstow would have been of short duration: river traffic up to Brockweir at the limit of the tidal range where the cargo would be broken down to smaller loads and transferred to shallow draught barges to be hauled still further upstream by men and horses. There would be coastal trading, cross-Channel trips and connections with the all important port of Bristol but the quayside here also marked the start of a long voyage for which no return tickets were issued. Not death, for that was at least a journey which the enforced travellers had had postponed, but transportation. A plaque on the Willow Tree Restaurant records their departure: The Chartists: From this riverside in 1840, John Frost, William Jones, Sarfanie Williams, the convicted leaders of the Chartist March on Newport, sailed to begin their transportation to Van Diemans Land, (Tasmania).

The fortunes made in the wine importing industry are apparent in the provision made by one man for the poor of the town. The inscription on the almshouses reads "...erected AD 1716 by the sole charity of Thomas Powys late of Enfield in the County of Middlesex, vintner, native of this town, for the reception and maintenance of 6 poor men and 6 poor women inhabitants of the town and parish for ever".

The inn sign of the oddly named Five Alls public house in Hocker Hill Street may raise a wry smile. Here depicted in the uniform of their professions we see a soldier, a bishop, a monarch, a barrister and finally the ordinary citizen characterised by John Bull. Beneath each is a short inscription: I fight for all, I pray for all,

I rule for all, I plead for all, and inevitably the last in line, I pay for all.

A man well remembered in Chepstow is William Williams, a hero of the war that was said to be the war to end all wars. William Williams, was an able seaman on his majesty's ship *River Clyde* during the ill-fated landing at Gallipoli on April 25, 1915. The plan was to place a number of smaller ships close to the shore to make a bridge over which the assault troops being disembarked from the transports could reach land. Not all these smaller ships reached their intended place leaving a gap. Commander Unwin and Able Seaman Williams plunged into the water with ropes to try to haul missing boats into position so that the landing could be effected as intended. All this took place under heavy fire but they persisted in their efforts, waist deep in water. Williams was killed before the ropes could be fully secured. He and others connected with this aspect of the assault were awarded Victoria Crosses. In Williams case, there was the added distinction of the first posthumous award to the Royal Navy. His story is told in both the museum and parish church.

The museum has much to tell of other aspects of the town's history, not the least the "Wye Tourists" who found the area so attractive - Men like William Gilpin, a noted travel writer of his day who published his "observations of the picturesque beauty" of the area. Many other writers and artists were greatly impressed by the romantic images they perceived and hastened to transfer their experiences to print and paper. In that respect times have not changed. Prints and quotations from the writings of this "Romantic Period" are to be found in the museum's print room. It makes an interesting comparison with the impressions of today's explorer and writer who may be encouraged in the belief that after all he is not "so over the top" as he sometimes supposes he might be.

Other exhibits include information on the netting of salmon and the basket traps that in essence ensured the fish died by drowning. Strange to record that fish can drown in their natural element, but this is the case. The salmon were held fast by their heads and, unable to escape, were killed by the water being forced through the gills.

Sometimes it is old notices that prove of special interest and I cite two that have been preserved. The first is in the form of an advertisement which, in the current thinking about alcohol, demonstrates that there is nothing new under the sun. Kingsfors and Rakes, St Annes Cider Works, proudly offered to supply "a new temperance and non-alcoholic drink called Champagne Cidrecoupe at two shillings per dozen plain bottles". It backed up its claim with a copy of Gloucestershire's public analyst's report dated December 1894 which said the cider contained only .33% alcohol by volume and the perry only .93%. The official must have been very impressed by the product for he felt moved to add a note: "I think you may congratulate yourselves in getting a very fine non-alcoholic beverage."

In 1865 four compositors went into print on their own accord in defence of their trade thus: "Reward More Yankee Brag. Whereas one Alfred Hillman, late jobbing compositor having had the unparalleled mendacity to issue a handbill wherein he styled himself the only practical printer and bookbinder in the neighbourhood, a reward of five shillings will be paid to any person producing his indentures or giving satisfactory information as to where and with whom he served his time to either printing or bookbinding. As this gasconading upstart must have well known he was uttering a unmitigated and barefaced falsehood in stating that he was the only practical printer in this neighbourhood. And we hereby caution the above named "gentleman of talent and position" to discontinue such impudent misstatements which are calculated to injure us and to mislead the public or we shall commence legal proceedings against him." Strong stuff, he surely touched a raw nerve and what a lovely expression, "gasconading upstart"! Not in everyday use but perhaps it will make a comeback - a gascon, the *Oxford English Dictionary* informs me, is a braggart, not a term to be applied to all hailing from that part of the world I am sure.

And so to Saint Mary's Church, a light and airy building that should not be missed with many features to capture the interest of even the most casual visitor. Most spectacular of several fine monuments is the highly coloured tomb of Henry, the Second Earl of Worcester, Lord Herbert of Chepstow, Raglan and Gower. His wife Elizabeth was the daughter of a Knight of the Garter, Sir Anthony Brown, standard bearer to Henry VIII. The couple lie here together in the splendour of their coronation robes.

Another example of the monumental mason's craft is to be found in the south transept "In memory of Thomas Shipman and Margaret his wife, daughter of John Maddock of Woolaston, gentleman, and their 12 children, also Richard Clayton Esq., who was married to Margaret relict of the above mentioned Thomas Shipman 1620". Gathered around them are the children in devotional attitudes and a reminder to us all: on the left of the tomb Old Father Time stands patiently waiting with scythe and hour glass. To the right, the sands of time having run out, death is depicted as a grim skeleton.

Close by is the mechanism of the church's eighteenth-century clock made locally by William Meredith in 1775, clearly an excellent craftsman for it served church and community for almost 200 years. It was man that tired, not the clock; the daily trip up the tower to wind up the weights came to an end when the hands were commanded to do their work by electricity. An appeal in 1858 for funds to repair the clock was made in verse form:

> *When Meredith first place me here:*
> *Of county clocks I was the peer:*
> *My voice was sweet my frame was bright:*
> *My pointers ever right and tight.*

Modern craftsmanship has a welcome place in the church with a large number of hand-embroidered commemorative kneelers, over fifty made by one lady of the parish. Over the baptistery is a tapestry by Anna Adam, 1988, showing Chepstow's bridge, castle and church with a symbolic dove.

Near the church doorway is the grave of Chepstow's prisoner in the tower, Henry Marten, whose signature, one of 59 on an historic document ensured his own eventual imprisonment. The document drawn at the High Court of Justice on January 29 1648 was no less than the warrant to execute King Charles the First on the following day. His life is recounted in a finely printed sheet together with an engraving from Coxe's *Monmouthshire* of 1801, the reproduction most excellently produced by a young apprentice from the Army School at Chepstow.

The King met his death publicly and bravely in Whitehall but on the restoration of the monarchy in 1660, Marten's days of freedom were at an end, although by all accounts he lived in some style and clearly was not subjected to any great hardship since he lived eight years beyond the allotted span of three score years and ten. Having rather more time at his disposal for thought than most he is said to have been the author of his own epitaph which takes the form of an acrostic:

Here or elsewhere (all's one to you and or me)
Earth, air or water gripes my ghostless duty
None knows how soon to be by fire set free
Reader, if you an oft tried rule will trust
You'll gladly do and suffer what you must
My life was spent in serving yours and you
And death's my pay (it seems) and welcome too
Revenge destroying but itself, while I
To birds of prey leave my old cage and fly.
Examples preach to the eye. Care then (mine says)
Not how you end, but how you spend your days.

Thus a link has been made with the town's finest and oldest building, the castle, which for over 900 years has dominated the town and the river.

Most walkers will make immediately for Chepstow Castle, but it has been deliberately left until the very end for in a way it symbolises our journey down the Wye; a journey characterised by the succession of strongholds from many ages, the hill forts of the native dwellers of this land of ours, the Roman station at Kenchester, the early motte and baileys succeeded by more substantial castles in stone of which Chepstow is the finest example.

We have seen something of its great strength from our look-out just before we forsook the wooded paths of the Wye Valley for the pavements of Chepstow. As fine a guardian of the river as you are likely to see, raised high on the sheer cliffs - unassailable from the water. It is, of course, Norman in origin, the first castle to be built in stone and improved on in the centuries following the Conquest. A great fortress, it was held by a succession of men from William fitz Osbern, who was responsible for the Great Tower of 1067 and who set the pattern for those who were to follow him. Each added to its strength as they improved its defences - a textbook in stone of military engineering and tactics. The gatehouse of 1225 was the work of the Marshall family, the entrance to the castle safeguarded by double gates and two portcullises. From here on we are in a world of the long siege, attack and defence tactics, with murder holes, arrow slits, barbicans, sally ports and fields of fire. A tradition that has an echo today, for the gates which now admit the tourist were made and installed by the young soldiers of the Army Apprentices School in 1964 - faithful iron-studded replicas, an impressive piece of work.

If Goodrich had great atmosphere then Chepstow surpasses it, the epitome of the might of the Norman chain of castles along the frontier of Wales - the iron hand in a stone glove. Here within this great stone fortress the blood tingles, the imagination races as you climb the tight spiral stone stairs or walk the ramparts and look down to the winding Wye. Today the ubiquitous jackdaws are the inheritors of the garrison of the castle, prototype for many a set created for film epics.

There must be countless stories to be told of the castle in days of both peace and conflict but two will suffice, one of a man killed and another of a man whose life was, remarkably, spared.

At the time of the bitter Civil War, the Earl of Worcester, a supporter of Charles I, held Chepstow and successfully resisted the Parliamentarian forces until 1645 but advances in the use of artillery had rendered the once impregnable walls susceptible to attack and its small body of defenders was forced into submission.

The resumption of hostilities in the following year found the Royalists back in possession under the command of Sir Nicholas Kemeys, but the artillery did its work only too well and once again the castle, isolated, fell to Cromwell's troops. Kemeys, a man of distinction as his commemorative plaque makes clear - "...knight and baronet of Cefn Mably and Llanviar Isoced, Member of Parliament, and High Sherrif of the counties of Monmouth and Glamorgan" was killed, apparently not in the attack but executed shortly after the surrender.

A man, for whom some might have said there was more justification for the death sentence, for he was guilty of regicide, survived for twenty years as a prisoner in a tower. Although built hundreds of years earlier by Roger Bigod III, it was destined to have the name of its most famous prisoner rather than its begetter assigned to it. He was Henry Marten, one of the many signatories to the death warrant of King Charles I. He lived here, apparently in some style, not alone but with the solace of female company and servants to attend upon him and was allowed out into the town on social visits. You may look from the glassless window to take in the prisoner's view of the castle. Perhaps scan the walls of his room to see if he, like many a prisoner, had scratched his name into the stone.

The days of castles were fading, many after the Civil War were slighted although Chepstow, so importantly positioned remained manned until 1690, when its guns were removed and sent to Chester.

Thus it is with the last and greatest in a chain of castles that we come to the end of our journey down the Wye.

30: Useful Information

Tourist Information Centres

(Note: not all offices are open throughout the year)

LLANIDLOES	Longbridge Street. 05512 2605
	for information for explorers north of Rhayader.
RHAYADER:	The Old Swan, West Street, Rhayader, Powys
	LD6 5AB 0597 810591
LLANDRINDOD WELLS	Town Hall,
	Llandrindod Wells, Powys LD1 6AA 0597 822600
BUILTH WELLS	Groe car park,
	Builth Wells, Powys LD2 3BL 0982 553307
HAY-ON-WYE	Main car park, Hay-on-Wye, Powys. 0497 820144
HEREFORD	Town Hall Annexe, St Owens Street,
	Hereford HR1 2PJ 0432 268430
ROSS-ON-WYE	Wyedean Tourist Board. 20 Broad Street,
	Ross-on-Wye HR9 7EA 0989 62768
MONMOUTH	Shire Hall, Monmouth, Gwent NP5 3BX 0600 3899
TINTERN	Tintern Abbey, Gwent NP6 6TE 0291 689431
CHEPSTOW	The Gate House, High St, Chepstow, Gwent NP6 5LH 02912 3772

Accommodation

Many tourist information centres have both lists and an advance booking service. They may also have details of bed and breakfast accommodation which may not appear in printed lists and can be helpful in assisting to find accommodation to suit your pocket.

The range of accommodation along the way is quite wide with a good choice to be found in the larger towns - Rhayader, Builth Wells, Hay-on-Wye, Hereford, Ross-on-Wye, Monmouth and Chepstow. Villages such as Erwood, Llandogo and Tintern also have a choice of bed and breakfast accommodation. For explorers of the Wye north of Rhayader a choice of accommodation can be found at Llangurig.

Published lists include:

POWYS COUNTY COUNCIL, has a short accommodation list covering the Rhayader to Hay-on-Wye section of the walk and obtainable from the Planning Dept, County Hall, Llandrindod Wells LD1 5LG.

HAY-ON-WYE TOURIST INFORMATION BUREAU has a useful list with accommodation in the town and surrounding villages including Glasbury, Llowes, Clyro, Clifford, Bredwardine.

HOLIDAYING IN HEREFORDSHIRE - a visitors' handbook available from the Hereford tourist information centre lists a variety of accommodation with a price guide.

ROSS-ON-WYE & DISTRICT Hoteliers & Caterers Association has an official guide (priced) with an accommodation list which can be obtained from the Wyedean Tourist Office.

Travel and Transport

RAIL: Nearest British Rail station to the northern end of the walk is Llandrindod Wells. The ten miles to Rhayader can be bridged by the bus service operated by Cross Gate Coaches or Postbus. Timetable enquiries: Llandrindod Wells (0597) 851226. (See also note about bus services generally.)

There are also British Rail stations at Hereford and at the end of the walk at Chepstow with full link to the national network.

ROAD: Bus services vary considerably, tending to get thinner as they move further away from the main towns so that a careful scrutiny of the timetables is needed if the route is to be walked in short hops.

RED & WHITE COACH AND BUS SERVICES

Timetables are available from Area Office Marches, Chepstow Depot, Bulwark, Chepstow, Gwent. NP6 5XZ. Travel enquiries (between 10.00am and 3.00pm Monday to Friday) Chepstow (02912) 622947 and Ross-on-Wye (0989) 62319.

EAST GWENT, SOUTH HEREFORD & WEST GLOUCESTERSHIRE

This timetable offers good travel possibilities in the lower Wye Valley for "bus out and walk back" expeditions.

HEREFORD AND WORCESTER AREA

At first sight the situation looks rather complicated due to the multiplicity of operators. The county council smooths the way with a comprehensive index and a whole raft of timetables together with a bus map. All are available from the Planning Dept, County Hall, Spetchley Road, Worcester WR5 2NP. A stamped addressed envelope is required. Local tourist offices and libraries also stock timetables for their areas.

POWYS

Again a complex situation but the county council co-ordinates the assembly of timetables (over a hundred including rail). Timetables are available for reference at public libraries, main post offices and tourist information offices. A bus and rail map is also available on request which lists operators, day services available, relevant timetable numbers and telephone numbers for enquiries. The county council will supply copies of individual timetables on request to County Hall, Llandrindod Wells. LD1 5LG - sae required. Powys is a sparsely populated area and understandably the services are often of a very limited nature - advance planning is essential. The table for the services operated by Roy Brown Coaches of Builth Wells may be helpful - enquiries Builth Wells (0982 552597); they also run a taxi service.

LONG DISTANCE COACHES

TRAWS CAMBRIA has a daily summer service across Wales Cardiff-Wrexham calling at Builth Wells and Llandrindod Wells. Enquiries Cardiff (0222 371331).

NATIONAL EXPRESS operates services into the area. For latest details contact your nearest depot or travel agent or Birmingham (021 622 4373).

YEOMANS CANYON TRAVEL of Hereford operates a one day a week service during June-August between Hereford and Aberystwyth via Kington, Rhayader and Llangurig. Enquiries (0432 356 201).

ROY BROWNS COACHES operates on selected days from Easter to the end of September between Rhayader and Aberystwyth via Llangurig and Plynlimon Restaurant. Enquiries (0982 552597).

TAXIS proved to be reasonably priced and with two passengers in some cases cost little more than the bus fare. Taxi services can be selected as and when required from the local tourist information offices. Some element of advance booking may be required in some areas as some are involved in hospital or school transport.

Table of Distances
(Note all distances quoted are approximately only.)

Rhayader	Miles	Cumulative		Miles	Cumulative
Newbridge	$9^{1}/_{2}$	$9^{1}/_{2}$	Mordiford	$5^{1}/_{2}$	$65^{1}/_{2}$
Builth Wells	7	$16^{1}/_{2}$	How Caple	$6^{1}/_{2}$	72
Erwood Bridge	$6^{1}/_{2}$	23	Ross-on-Wye	$5^{1}/_{2}$	$77^{1}/_{2}$
Glasbury	9	32	Kerne Bridge	$5^{1}/_{4}$	$82^{3}/_{4}$
Hay-on-Wye	5	37	Yat Rock	$5^{1}/_{4}$	88
Bredwardine	9	46	Monmouth	$7^{1}/_{2}$	$95^{1}/_{2}$
Kenchester	7	53	Tintern	$11^{1}/_{2}$	107
Hereford	7	60	Chepstow	5	112

Places to visit on and around the Wye Valley Walk
(Note: Opening times are provided for guidance only and should be verified if a special visit is intended.)

ELAN VALLEY VISITOR CENTRE Summer 10.00am-6.00pm. Closes end October.

RHAYADER MUSEUM, EAST STREET Varying days Easter to end of September.

THE WIER GARDEN, SWAINSHILL, Nr. HEREFORD National Trust. Mid-February to end October.Wed-Sun plus Bank Holiday Mondays. 11.00am-6.00pm. A spring delight with fine views of the Wye.

HEREFORD
Broomy Hill Engines. Limited opening, check with tourist information centre.
Cathedral. Daily.
Cider Museum. April to October daily 10.00am-5.30pm. November to March Mon-Sat 1.00-5.00pm.
Churchill Gardens Museum. Check at tourist information centre for opening times according to season.
City Museum & Art Gallery.   ditto.
The Old House.   ditto.
St. John's Mediaeval Museum.   ditto.
Railway Centre. April/September weekends and Bank Holidays special steam days.
Note there are also conducted tours of the city during the summer. Check with the tourist information office.

MONMOUTH
Nelson Museum. Daily. Closes for lunch.
Afternoons only on Sunday.

TINTERN ABBEY Winter: Weekdays 9.30am-4.00pm
Sundays 2.00pm-4.00pm
Closed Christmas Eve, Christmas Day and New Year's Day.
Summer: End March - mid-October.
Daily 9.30am-7.00pm. Last admission 6.30pm.

CHEPSTOW
Castle. Daily from 9.30am. Sunday from 2.00pm.
Museum. Daily from March to October from 11.00am, extended opening in July/August. Sundays from 2.00pm.

There are many other attractions close to the route of the Wye Valley Walk which are too numerous to list here.

Printed by
Carnmor Print & Design, London Road, Preston